T0195691

FROM SALVATION *to* SERVICE

DAILY WALKING WITH GOD

JOYE ANGEL

WESTBOW
PRESS®
A DIVISION OF THOMAS NELSON
& ZONDERVAN

WestBow Press books may be ordered through booksellers or by contacting:

WestBow Press
A Division of Thomas Nelson & Zondervan
1663 Liberty Drive
Bloomington, IN 47403
www.westbowpress.com
844-714-3454

Requests for information should be sent to
HOPE Ministries
2911hopeministries@gmail.com
www.joyelangel.com
www.myhopeministries.com

Scripture quotations are taken from the New King James Version®. Copyright © 1982 by Thomas Nelson. Used by permission. All rights reserved.

ISBN: 978-1-6642-7728-1 (sc)
ISBN: 978-1-6642-7729-8 (hc)
ISBN: 978-1-6642-7727-4 (e)

Library of Congress Control Number: 2022916154

Print information available on the last page.

WestBow Press rev. date: 08/30/2022

CONTENTS

ACKNOWLEDGMENTS

My Center Hill Church family: thank you for being a shining example of the love of Jesus.

Bro. Steve Havener and Bro. Kevin Angel: thank you for your guidance on this journey.

Hope Smith: thank you for always being there and saying yes to all my adventures!

Shaye Angel: thank you for always supporting me.

INTRODUCTION

Breathe it in. Today is a new day. It is the first day of the best part of your life. You have accepted Jesus Christ as your Lord and Savior. Welcome to the family!

I am sure you have lots of questions and would like a little guidance on what comes next.

Well, you have stopped at the right book! I have been where you are, and my prayer is that this book will help fill in the gaps. This is not an all-inclusive list for a life with God, but it will give you a starting point.

Now, let us start walking through life with the Lord. If you have never experienced salvation, my prayer is that you will not put it off another second. Let today be your day to start a life with God! Salvation is a gift that is offered freely to all. Salvation involves repentance, which is the turning away from sin. Every person is given the measure of faith for salvation, faith to accept Jesus Christ as Lord and Savior of our lives.

There is no salvation apart from a personal faith in Jesus Christ.

"But God demonstrates His own love toward us, in that while we were still sinners, Christ died for us" (Romans 5:8).

"For all have sinned and fall short of the glory of God" (Romans 3:23).

"For the wages of sin is death, but the gift of God is eternal life in Christ Jesus our Lord" (Romans 6:23).

"For He made Him who knew no sin to *be* sin for us, that we might become the righteousness of God in Him" (2 Corinthians 5:21).

"That if you confess with your mouth the Lord Jesus and believe in your heart that God has raised Him from the dead, you will be saved. For with the heart one believes unto righteousness, and with the mouth confession is made unto salvation" (Romans 10:9–10).

Are you ready to accept the gift of eternal life that Jesus is offering you right now? If it is your sincere desire to receive Jesus into your heart as your personal Lord and Savior, then talk to God from your heart.

There is no perfect prayer of salvation. It is just admitting that you are a sinner in need of a Savior, believing in your heart that Jesus died on the cross for your sins and that God raised Him from the dead, and confessing Jesus as Lord and Savior of your life.

You now have a friend, a confidant, a heavenly Father to stand by your side from this moment forward. One who desires a relationship with you. One who wants the best for your life. One who has a plan, a journey ready just for you.

Join us on this journey! A life walking with God is the most fulfilled life.

WHO IS GOD?

Life is possible because of the Creator of the universe. He is God. Let me offer you the biblical explanation of who God is. (At the end of this explanation I will list the scriptures in the Bible where you can search these for yourself.)

He is the Alpha and Omega, the beginning and the end. Everything that has ever been and ever will be is because of Him. He is the Creator of the world. He spoke the world into existence. He is love. He is forgiveness. He is grace. He is the godhead of the Trinity. The Trinity is God the Father, God the Son, and God the Holy Spirit. Each has a role in the life of a Christian. He knitted every person in the world together in the womb. He knew you before you knew yourself. He created you for a purpose. He draws you for salvation. He sent His Son to die on the cross to be the substitute for everyone so that we all would have a way to spend eternity in heaven with Him. He made the law. He gave Moses the Ten Commandments. He foreknew that we could not keep the law, so He extended grace through salvation.

He freely gives the Holy Spirit to all who accept salvation. Through the Holy Spirit, we gain the third person of the Trinity. We have access to everything; it is up to us how much we use it. He gives forgiveness to all who seek it with a humble heart. He sees your actions, and He knows your heart. He is omnipresent (everywhere at the same time), omniscient (all-knowing), omnipotent (all-powerful), and omnibenevolent (all-loving). He walks with every believer who allows Him to and guides their lives.

He has a plan for your life. He knows you personally. He gives gifts and talents to every person. He gives people free will. He longs to have a relationship with you. God made us to have a relationship with Him. You have an emptiness inside you that is filled when you accept salvation. As you grow your relationship with Him, your life is filled to overflowing.

"And He said to me, 'It is done! I am the Alpha and the Omega, the Beginning and the End. I will give of the fountain of the water of life freely to him who thirsts'" (Revelation 21:6).

"All things were made through Him, and without Him nothing was made that was made" (John 1:3).

"Before I formed you in the womb I knew you; before you were born I sanctified you; I ordained you a prophet to the nations" (Jeremiah 1:5).

"No one can come to Me unless the Father who sent Me draws him; and I will raise him up at the last day" (John 6:44).

"Jesus said to him, 'I am the way, the truth, and the life. No one comes to the Father except through Me'" (John 14:6).

"Then the Lord said to Moses, 'Come up to Me on the mountain and be there; and I will give you tablets of stone, and the law and commandments which I have written, that you may teach them'" (Exodus 24:12).

"Then Peter said to them, 'Repent, and let every one of you be baptized in the name of Jesus Christ for the remission of sins; and you shall receive the gift of the Holy Spirit'" (Acts 2:38).

"The eyes of the Lord are in every place, keeping watch on the evil and the good" (Proverbs 15:3).

"But Jesus looked at them and said to them, 'With men this is impossible, but with God all things are possible'" (Matthew 19:26).

"But God, who is rich in mercy, because of His great love with which He loved us, even when we were dead in trespasses, made us alive together with Christ (by grace you have been saved)" (Ephesians 2:4–5).

"There is no fear in love; but perfect love casts out fear, because fear involves torment. But he who fears has not been made perfect in love. We love Him because He first loved us" (1 John 4:18–19).

"For I know the thoughts that I think toward you, says the Lord, thoughts of peace and not of evil, to give you a future and a hope" (Jeremiah 29:11).

"Every good gift and every perfect gift is from above, and comes down from the Father of lights, with whom there is no variation or shadow of turning" (James 1:17).

"Oh, give thanks to the Lord, for He is good! For His mercy endures forever" (Psalm 136:1).

Life is surprising and frustrating—sometimes at the same time. I rarely know what God has planned for me. Most of the time when something comes up, I feel the Spirit leading me and know what the right choice is. That has led me to places I never thought I would go and into circumstances where I was not sure what would happen next. Every time, God was right there—through the frustration. Through the doors slammed shut. Through the choices I made. Through my questioning Him over whether I had made the right move. Through all the obstacles and past the point of giving up, He was there, each time, to pick me back up and get me back on the path.

Every mountaintop. Every surprise. Every new adventure. Every open door. Every step on the pathway. Every step, God was right there. God has taken me to amazing places. I have done things that I would have never thought I could, but with God, it has all been possible.

I trust that He will be with me always and that He will walk with me through every situation and circumstance, but I am still flesh. On these journeys, I have messed up and I have questioned God. I fell down and lay there. God is so good and gracious that He stayed right beside me. I will admit I had to be yanked up and kicked back on the path a time or two. He is still molding me. Through this walk with God, I move easier now and question Him less. I have walked this way for so long that I know I will not see the road ahead, and at times, the things I do will not make sense. I cannot see the full path. I do not see the pitfalls that He protects me from. I do not see the heartaches I never had to endure. Each day God goes before me, planning my way. All He asks is that I trust and follow Him.

This does not mean I will not endure hardships. Unfortunately, I have learned that the closer you become to God, the more the evil one notices you. The great thing about it is that with a closer relationship with God, I recognize earlier when the evil one is trying to invade and knock me down. I can see more clearly the stumbling blocks that are thrown at me. Of course, this does not mean that I do not still stumble and fall, but it is less often than it used to be. I am learning to step over the stumbling blocks instead of falling over them. I am a work in progress.

I know that I would not be where I am today without the guidance of God. I quit making plans for my life because where I am now was never something I thought I would do or a place I thought I would be. So I would have no clue where to go from here if I did make plans. A life with God is the most fulfilling experience, living day by day full of love for yourself and others, looking at the world and seeing the possibilities of what it could be, not what it currently is. Knowing that God loves every person, Christian or not, and has a plan for all their lives if they would just follow Him. It is reassuring to know that there is still an amazing amount of good in this world. It may be buried deep inside people, but it is still there.

"Thank you" are words that we do not use as often as we should. We often take for granted that God is always going to be there and will continue to bless us, regardless of our service for Him. That is not how a relationship with God should be. When we rise every morning, we should be thankful that the Lord gave us another day on this earth. We should strive to use those days to tell others about Him and His love. We should be thankful that we get to go to church. There are so many people who long for a church home and so many people who are homebound and do not have the opportunity to have fellowship with a church family. Those of us who do have an opportunity to worship the Lord in a body of believers should be very thankful. It is that recharge that we need to face a new week. There is nothing quite like being surrounded by those who lift you up, support you, and love you unconditionally.

We should be thankful that He does not give up on us. We push back, dig in, and run in the other direction, but He is patient with our rebellious ways. I would have given up on myself by now, but not God. He is still working on me. I would have given up on the world by now, but not God. He knows that there are still people out there who are willing to listen and hear His voice. People who are waiting on Christians to stop running and start telling others about Jesus so they can get saved. He sees the good in the world and He sees the good in us.

We should be thankful that He chose us. He chose you and me to spend eternity with Him in heaven. He chose you before you ever chose Him. He sent His Son to die on the cross for our sins to make a way that we can spend eternity with Him. He loves us so much that He made the ultimate sacrifice. That is love. That is something to be thankful for every day.

We should be thankful for our gifts and talents. God gave them to us. He handpicked you for a purpose and gave you the tools you need to accomplish that purpose. How amazing is it to know that He entrusted you so much that He gave you a calling? One specific to your life. One that He wants you to accomplish.

Life more abundant begins with service for the Lord. Through your service, you experience growth. Growth leads to a closer relationship with the Lord. A closer relationship means you feel more loved, more fulfilled, more settled, and more grounded. I cannot think of anyone who does not want those feelings in his or her life. It is available to anyone and everyone. Call on the name of the One who loves you more than you could ever love yourself and surrender your life to Him.

There are questions I get now more than ever: What if God is not real? What if you pass from this life only to find out you were wrong?

I can tell you God is real because I feel the Holy Spirit guiding me. I know He is real and that I have not wasted my life following a false religion.

However, for the sake of truly answering the question, here are my thoughts. Everything about God is love and service. That is how

I have lived my life. So if I pass from this life and determine that I am wrong, I have still lived a really good life. I have helped people. I have loved people. I have served others. And I would not change a thing. My life is filled to bubbling over because of my walk and my service. That is a pretty good life. Some of you are saying, "Well, I have lived the same kind of life." That is great, but you are missing the peace that comes from a walk with God. A peace that surpasses all understanding."

Service is not just about action; it also has to do with attitude. Remember when you were a child and were told to clean your room? As you went stomping off to the room and threw your toys around, the room really did not get cleaned up. And you could not understand why your parents were so mad; the toys were off of the floor. If you had gone into the room with a better attitude, everything would have been picked up and put in its place all nice and neat, and you would not have kept getting in trouble. That is what I mean when I say it has to do with attitude.

If you only help people because you feel obligated, you do not feel blessed about your service. The person you helped feels like a burden, and neither of you want to revisit this situation again. If you help people because you feel led to and truly with a heart of service, then you not only attend to their needs, you have their ear to speak with them about Jesus. You have the opportunity to be part of someone else's growth, salvation, walk, and more. Your walk is now intertwined with his or hers. You showed someone the love of Christ and allowed your light to shine brightly. This is a heart of service. Attitude can make all of the difference. If your service could use an adjustment in attitude, it is time to meet with the Lord and get to the root of the problem.

There are several reasons that our service could be suffering. One of the most common is that we did not involve God in the first place. We branched out on our own, without being led, and attempted service for God. See, God has to be in our service. We have to include

Him. This means we have to do the service that He has called us to do, not the service we want to do.

Let me illustrate this point. You wake up one morning and decide, on your own, that you will be a pastor. You think you are a good speaker and want to serve God. You determine that this must be the way. You contact another Christian to help and tell them that you are to be a pastor. Before you know it, you have worked your way into a church. No one listens to you at business meetings, and you are getting frustrated. You found these sermons on the internet and they sounded good, so you started using them every week, but no one came down during invitation, and the Spirit of the Lord was not in your church. You were pushed to the point and finally had a breakthrough: God did not tell you to be a pastor; this was not your calling.

I have seen it so many times, and I myself have done it; we run out ahead of God. We are so excited to serve Him. We are on fire and ready to see souls get saved.

What are the benefits of believing in and following God? You live your life thinking you are basically a good person. You have not broken any laws, or gotten any tickets, and you give to those in need. That is great!

But how is your life? How do you feel? Does it feel like something is missing and you are always working to fill that spot in your life? That is the way it was for me. I always felt in my heart that there had to be more to life than what I was doing. Yes, I tried to live my definition of a good person but always felt that I came up short. I did not see the bigger picture. This feeling kept nagging at me that life was not supposed to be this way.

Then I met Jesus and He changed my life. Now, I know that I am a good person because of the cleansing power of Jesus Christ, not anything that I have done but what He has done through me. So, if you feel that life is about being good and doing good, then life with God is for you. You will still live a life being good and doing good, but with God on your side, your life is better and your service is better. I love my life with God.

A life with God means a hope for the future. You see the good in the world and know how good the world can be. You have a love for others that you never had before. You care about other people and their future. Life might still be frustrating at times, but with God, you know there is hope for a better tomorrow. When you have a hope for the future, you look forward to your tomorrows.

When you accept salvation, it does not mean you sit down and that is all there is to life. If that were the case, God would take you to heaven as soon as you prayed the sinner's prayer. There is work to be done. He has a calling on each one of our lives. Our very first calling is to tell others about Him. Right now, you are probably shaking your head no and scared to open your mouth. God will put the words into your mouth just like He did for Jeremiah.

> "Then the Lord put forth His hand and touched my mouth, and the Lord said to me: 'Behold, I have put my words in your mouth'" (Jeremiah 1:9).

If you completely trust in Him, then you trust that He will take care of you. Simply put, open your mouth and see what happens. I remember the first time I talked with someone about Jesus. I was so nervous I heard my heart beating in my ears. I do not remember any of the conversation, just how I felt. Walking away, I remember thinking that it was not as bad as I thought it was going to be. The next time was easier, and then the next easier, and now I talk about God all the time. He is my main topic of conversation.

When I come across someone who is adamantly against God, I find myself trying to make a conscious effort with my words and tone down my God talk so he or she does not leave the conversation. I never want people to leave thinking they were not heard, but they will not leave until they hear about God; sometimes you have to be more delicate than others. For me, that does not come naturally, so God is still molding that part of me.

You will find the same with you. Quit shaking your head. Start growing your relationship with God and ask that He give you the boldness to speak with others about Him. It will happen. God is faithful, and you will see that talking about God is not as hard as you think. You have the Holy Spirit that guides, so lean on Him for direction, and trust that God will put the words in your mouth.

A life with God means hope for eternity. This life passes by so quickly. The days seem to go faster and faster. One day we will all pass from this life, if God does not return beforehand. Once that happens, there is more than just the life you lived here on earth. The hope is to spend eternity in heaven with God. That hope gives every believer a wonderful eternal life to look forward to.

Looking at God from a biblical standpoint, we can see where God created everything and is over everything and everyone, guiding us through this life. Now, let us look at God from a creation standpoint. The theory is that there was a big bang that brought the world into existence. According to scientists, astronomers, and cosmologists, the universe as we know it was created in a massive explosion that not only created the majority of matter but physical laws that govern our ever-expanding cosmos.

In short, the Big Bang Theory states that all the current and past matter in the universe came into existence at the same time, roughly 13.8 billion years ago. While Christianity and scientists do not normally agree, when you take a closer look, you might think differently.

In his article, "A Christian Physicist Examines the Big Bang Theory," Dr. Steven Ball concluded that the Big Bang Theory confirms the validity of the Bible. The Bible clearly explains in Genesis that God created the heavens and the earth, that God spoke the world into existence. I think we can all agree that the universe was formed approximately fourteen billion years ago. I have not found anyone who wants to argue that point.

However, the earth, which is the only planet habitable by people and animals, actually came into existence around four billion years ago. Apparently, the universe and galaxies had to be formed to pave the way for a planet like the earth to be formed. The sun and the moon had to be set so that the sun could warm the waters and the moon could stabilize the rotation of the earth. All these ripples, as they are called, had to happen for the earth's formation. This is science and scripture lining up. If you look at elements of the Big Bang Theory, you can line them up with the scriptures of creation.

In the end, we are not that different. We have all been on the same path and reached similar conclusions. We do differ on the responsibility for creation. For me, there is only one answer, which is God. The work that went into every detail of the earth shows His love for creation. The sustainability of everything on this planet shows His care. I choose to believe that there is a force at work that is greater than anything on this planet. Most people agree with that. I choose to believe that this force is God.

The point I am trying to make is that science and Christianity do not have to compete. It is not a question of who is right and who is wrong. We are all looking for the same answers. Scientists take a theory and study it out. Many painstaking hours go into each experiment. For the ones that yield results, there are hundreds more that did not. That makes each paper or article published so precious.

Theology is the study of the nature of God and religious belief. Christians who study theology dive deep into scriptures looking beyond what is written in the Bible and looking to historical and scientific evidence. These theologians study and compare the evidence until coming to a conclusion. See the similarities? Both are passionate about the same thing—the study of the universe and everything in it.

Now, for me, I just take it on faith. The scripture says it, so I choose to believe it. That is the type of person I am. I think theology and science are both fascinating, and I have immense respect for those in their fields. Even though we are different people, God made us all, and we are all fulfilling that purpose.

The real question, the most important question, is what do we do with our knowledge? Do we keep everything we have learned to ourselves? When a scientist makes a discovery, papers are published, books are written, and talks are given on the subject matter.

You have made the most important discovery of your life—Jesus Christ. Now that you have Jesus in your life, you cannot keep that to yourself. You may not be comfortable shouting it from the rooftops or marching down the street with a megaphone, but you get the idea. Telling others.

There is a world full of people who are looking and searching for the "next" thing, the thing that will fill the void in their lives. The thing that will satisfy for the moment. But we have good news; that void can be filled permanently. Having a personal relationship with Jesus Christ satisfies that longing for eternity. What better news could a world hear than that? Oh wait—and it is free! Jesus paid the price for your salvation; all you have to do is surrender and accept it. Realize that you do not have to walk through this life alone. You have a Father who loves you and wants to have a relationship with you. We should strive every day to talk to someone about God.

2

DECISION

We have moments when we do not feel deserving of love or that we are unworthy. It can be hard to allow God to love you, to allow God to show you that you are loved, you are adored, you are chosen, you are set apart. You are enough just as you are. God is calling you to a relationship—no judgment, no condemnation—just love and forgiveness. Open your heart to Jesus today. Do not turn away. Let yourself be loved with the everlasting love of Jesus.

You have felt the pull of God. You know there is a force greater than ourselves at work around us. You have felt the love encompass you. You surrendered your life to Jesus Christ and accepted His free gift of salvation. Maybe you walked the aisle at church or said the prayer sitting in your pew. Maybe you were at home by yourself or talking with a friend. Salvation can happen anytime and anywhere. There is no designated time and place to accept salvation. The only thing that matters is that you do not deny the pull of God and accept salvation.

I was saved at age thirteen. The Lord had been heavily dealing with me. I was visiting my grandmother's house and was full of questions. My grandmother had just finished telling me her salvation story. I was in the bathroom brushing my teeth, and the feeling was so strong that I stopped mid-brush and prayed the prayer right there. It felt like I could not waste another second without Jesus in my heart. What an amazing feeling washed over me. I knew from that point forward that I was a child of God. Of course, I finished brushing my teeth and left the bathroom praising my risen Savior. It was an amazing feeling to know I was loved so completely.

Ok, so I am a Christian—now what?

First, you need to start reading the Word of the Lord. The Bible is your life guide. Your instruction manual. It is referred to as the Living Word. The Bible is an important part of our Christian life. Whether you purchase an actual Bible or get a Bible app, start reading. You will find that the Bible comes in many translations. Do not be overwhelmed because you are not sure which one to choose. Try out verses on the internet or a Bible app and change the translation to see how differently the words read. Find a translation you are comfortable with. Remember, just because you choose one translation today does not mean you have to stick to that translation tomorrow. I own several Bibles with different translations. Each one served a purpose in a period of my life. You can get all that through an app now and have every translation at your fingertips. You can also use BibleGateway. com, there are tons of translations available on that site as well.

Now, you have decided on a translation. If you are purchasing a Bible, remember, there are a lot of different options, so take your time and look through each one. Large print, indexed, reference, study— choose the options that are right for you. There is no reason to rush this purchase. Make sure you get one that will work for you. After you have made your purchase, it is time to start reading.

When you start reading, start with the New Testament. This will give you a better understanding of the life of Jesus and what He went through for you. The first four books of the New Testament are referred to as the Gospels. They are Matthew, Mark, Luke, and John. These four books recount the life of Jesus Christ. They tell of His birth, life, and death on the cross. Each book is slightly different and offers a different emphasis. They are all equally good. The Gospels also tell of the ministry of Jesus, and we see examples of how we are to live in the life of Jesus.

One of the most recognized verses is in these first four books. Of course, I am talking about John 3:16, but have you ever read the verses that come after?

> "For God so loved the world that He gave His only begotten Son, that whoever believes in Him should not perish but have everlasting life. For God did not send His Son into the world to condemn the world, but that the world through Him might be saved.
>
> He who believes in Him is not condemned; but he who does not believe is condemned already because he has not believed in the name of the only begotten Son of God. And this is the condemnation, that the light has come into the world, and men loved darkness rather than light, because their deeds were evil. For everyone practicing evil hates the light and does not come to the light, lest his deeds should be exposed. But he who does the truth comes to the light, that his deeds may be clearly seen, that they have been done in God." (John 3:16–21)

Be a lover of the light, for you have not been condemned but saved by God's amazing grace. Practice and seek truth in all things. Stay away from evil; it will drag you into the darkness. God does not want the world to be condemned; it is His desire that all be saved. Is it not wonderful to see what can be learned from just a few verses? God loves you and wants you to spend eternity in heaven with Him.

Why is the Bible important? Why should you want to read the Bible?

"All Scripture is given by inspiration of God, and is profitable for doctrine, for reproof, for correction, for instruction in righteousness, that the man of God may be complete, thoroughly equipped for every good work" (2 Timothy 3:16–17).

All Scripture is God's Word. That is why it is referred to as the Living Word. God reveals things to us through the verses. I can have a heavy burden in my life and sit down to read my Bible. God will lead me to the verses that apply to my situation and give me the reassurance needed to ease my burdens. I can also read the same verses in different situations in my life and receive different revelations each time. My grandmother continually read through the Bible for this very reason. Each time she read, God revealed different things to her. She was always learning and growing in the Lord.

How do you grow in your faith and expand your knowledge?

"Therefore, laying aside all malice, all deceit, hypocrisy, envy, and all evil speaking, as newborn babes, desire the pure milk of the word, that you may grow thereby, if indeed you have tasted that the Lord is gracious" (1 Peter 2:1–3).

The Bible referenced the milk of the Word. Just like a baby, you are considered a babe in Christ and start on the pure milk so that you can grow and move on to the meat of the Word. The Lord is gracious to us by providing the availability of the Bible to everyone. Even those that have not experienced salvation can read the Word of the Lord, it is not just for the Christians. If you have an interest in learning more about Jesus or the Christian life, then the Bible is for you.

As we grow in our relationship with Christ, we grow in knowledge. Knowledge leads to trust and faithfulness. Trust leads to taking that first step of faith. Before you know it, you are walking through life side by side with the Lord.

Remember that we have to remain diligent. The Christian life is not easy. We are surrounded on every side by the world, but we are called to be different. To be a light to the world to show everyone the love of Jesus Christ. It is important to set aside time every day to read the Word of the Lord and soak up knowledge.

"Let us therefore be diligent to enter that rest, lest anyone fall according to the same example of disobedience. For the word of God is living and powerful, and sharper than any two-edged sword, piercing even to the division of soul and spirit, and of joints and marrow, and is a discerner of the thoughts and intents of the heart." (Hebrews 4:11–12)

As we grow in knowledge and become closer to God, we realize this life we are walking, with God, is the best life. It is such a wonderful feeling to have that fulfillment in your life. No matter the circumstances, no matter the situations, God is always there.

"But grow in the grace and knowledge of our Lord and Savior Jesus Christ" (2 Peter 3:18).

Being a Christian is so much more than going to church or just proclaiming that we are a Christian. Being a Christian means that we live for Christ every day. We set ourselves apart from the world. We work daily to sin less. Many times, I hear about the things that you have to give up to be a Christian. I did not necessarily give up those things after becoming a Christian, I did not have the same desires that I did before. So it was not really giving something up if you do not want it anymore. A good example of that is when growing up, I loved ice cream. I probably could have had ice cream with every meal. As an adult, I do not have the same feeling toward ice cream anymore, so it is easy not to even think about it.

We grow and we change. A life with the Lord is growth and

change. I do not miss the life I had before I knew God. My only regret is that I did not start my service sooner so I could have had a longer relationship with the Lord. My daily prayer is less of me and more of the Lord. My desire is to follow Him wherever He leads.

> "Then Jesus said to His disciples, "If anyone desires to come after Me, let him deny himself, and take up his cross, and follow Me. For whoever desires to save his life will lose it, but whoever loses his life for My sake will find it." (Matthew 16:24–25)

We have received God's amazing grace through salvation. Undeserved, but freely given. Now that you have accepted this free gift, it is your turn to tell others about the love of Jesus and how He can change their lives like He changed yours.

3

BAPTISM

Baptism is the immersion of a person into the water and rising again. The immersion in water is a symbolism of the death, burial, and resurrection of Jesus Christ. When we are baptized, we symbolize that our old life is washed away and we rise anew. Baptism is from the Greek work *baptizo,* meaning to immerse, to submerge.

After we accept salvation, baptism is the next step. This step is the public showing of your faith, announcing to the world that you are a Christian. There are many people who do not believe that baptism serves any purpose. I accepted salvation at thirteen but was not baptized until I was an adult. I felt something missing in my life. I was so blessed to be baptized by my husband. When I came out of the water, life felt different. I felt different.

At that point I chose to go in a different direction—to follow the Lord. Baptism made a difference in my life. Baptism did not save me. Salvation did that. Baptism is your first step of obedience, of faith.

If you have never been baptized, open your mind and heart to consider it. Even Jesus Himself was baptized by John the Baptist in the Jordan River. There are many instances in the Bible that speak of baptism. Paul was baptized. Lydia's family was baptized. The jailer was baptized. The list goes on.

The best reason to say yes to baptism is that the Lord asks you to do it. Even if it has been years since your salvation, you can be baptized. It does not negate your salvation or your faith in Jesus. It has the opposite result. Baptism brings you closer to the Lord.

Churches have different schedules and procedures for baptism. Talk with your pastor or church leader and ask to be baptized. Then tell your story. Baptism is a picture of your devotion and commitment to Jesus Christ. It is not optional in a life with God. If it was important enough that Jesus Christ was baptized, it is also important for you to follow in baptism.

4

PRAYER

The thing I hear most often from Christians is about their prayer life or lack thereof. Understanding the basics of prayer and how to have a more effective, fervent prayer life is extremely important. I call prayer our telephone to God, so knowing how to effectively communicate is essential.

The Bible even offers us a model prayer in Matthew 6. If you do not know what to pray, start here.

> "In this manner, therefore, pray: Our Father in heaven, Hallowed be Your name. Your kingdom come. Your will be done on earth as it is in heaven. Give us this day our daily bread. And forgive us our debts, as we forgive our debtors. And do not lead us into temptation, but deliver us from the evil one. For Yours is the kingdom and the power and the glory forever. Amen." (Matthew 6:9–13)

Prayer is your personal communication line to God. It is your chance to come before your heavenly Father, to be in His presence, to humble yourself and praise the Lord.

The ACTS (adoration, confession, thanksgiving, supplication) prayer model is a standard that helps teach the parts of prayer.

- The A stands for adoration, which is paying honor to God for who He is.
- The C stands for confession—confessing your sins and asking for forgiveness.
- The T stands for thanksgiving, thanking God for all He has done.
- The S stands for supplication, which is bringing your needs and the needs of others to God.

In Nehemiah 9:4–38, God's people spent twenty-eight verses praising Him and thanking Him before they asked for anything. That is how you focus on God in prayer and really connect with Him.

Now, my prayers are in a different order, I use ATCS, but do not feel you have to follow this exactly; it is just a guide to help make your prayer life more personal.

Several scriptures can help to get your heart ready for prayer. This is one of my favorites.

> "Make a joyful shout to the Lord, all you lands! Serve the Lord with gladness; Come before His presence with singing. Know that the Lord, He is God; It is He who has made us, and not we ourselves; we are His people and the sheep of His pasture. Enter into His gates with thanksgiving and into His courts with praise. Be thankful to Him, and bless His name. For the Lord is good; His mercy is everlasting, and His truth endures to all generations." (Psalm 100:1–5)

We begin prayer by recognizing who God is and thanking Him for what He has done. Next is the condition of your heart. Do you pray with just your mind, or does your heart desire a close relationship with God? That is something you will have to search out and discover. "Confession is good for the soul" is not just a saying. Confessing your sins before Almighty God cleanses you and makes you fit to pray.

Now, do you truly trust God? When you pray and ask God for something in your life or someone else's life, you have to give it to God and let Him handle it. After you turn it over to Him, do not pick it back up. You have to trust that He has the best plan for your life.

If you truly trust His leadership, then know that in Isaiah 55:8–9 it says,

> "'For My thoughts are not your thoughts, Nor are your ways My ways,' says the Lord. 'For as the heavens are higher than the earth, so are My ways higher than your ways, and My thoughts than your thoughts.'"

His way is always better.

Lastly, you must set aside a time and place to pray. Mine is first thing in the morning. If you make a schedule, it is easier to make this your routine so that when you get busy, you will not forget to pray. Whether it is morning, noon, or night, set aside a time that works with your schedule even if that means rising earlier in the morning or changing your lunch plans. Prayers are important. Bring what you need with you to your prayer time: Bible, prayer journal, devotion, whatever helps you. Then, start your prayer, wait for the Holy Spirit, and see what a difference a few changes in your prayer life can make.

Work to strengthen your prayer life so that you will have a place shaking prayer, as the disciples did in Acts.

> "So when they heard that, they raised their voice to God with one accord and said: "Lord, You are God, who made heaven and earth and the sea, and all that is in them, who by the mouth of Your servant David have said:

'Why did the nations rage,
And the people plot vain things?
The kings of the earth took their stand,
and the rulers were gathered together
against the Lord and against His Christ.'

"'For truly against Your holy Servant Jesus, whom You anointed, both Herod and Pontius Pilate, with the Gentiles and the people of Israel, were gathered together to do whatever Your hand and Your purpose determined before to be done. Now, Lord, look on their threats, and grant to Your servants that with all boldness they may speak Your word, by stretching out Your hand to heal, and that signs and wonders may be done through the name of Your holy Servant Jesus.'"

And when they had prayed, the place where they were assembled together was shaken; and they were all filled with the Holy Spirit, and they spoke the word of God with boldness." (Acts 4:24–31)

Throughout the Bible, you see the importance of prayer. All the heroes of faith fought their battles on their knees. You have to get connected with the Father to know His will. You have to stay connected to the Father and allow Him to guide your steps daily.

In 1 Kings, when Elijah took a stand against Ahab and Jezebel, he could not have done so without the power of prayer. Elijah did not have the power to withhold the rain from the earth. The Lord is the one that withheld the rain for three and a half years.

"And Elijah the Tishbite, of the inhabitants of Gilead, said to Ahab, 'As the Lord God of Israel lives, before whom I stand, there shall not be dew nor rain these years, except at my word'" (1 Kings 17:1).

As we read on into 1 Kings 18, we see that Elijah was faithful and when the Lord came to him, even though the other prophets were in hiding fearing for their lives, Elijah went to Ahab. The Bible does not say much about how Elijah felt or what he thought, just that he went. I imagine Elijah could not help but think about the fate of the prophets who lost their lives or the prophets in hiding. However, Elijah trusted in the Lord and knew that even if he lost his earthly life, he would remain faithful to the Lord.

Having that close relationship with God brings a peace that surpasses all understanding and gives you the confidence to know that you might not be able to handle the tasks ahead, but He can, and He will accomplish them through you. You just have to be a willing servant.

> "And it came to pass after many days that the word of the Lord came to Elijah, in the third year, saying, 'Go, present yourself to Ahab, and I will send rain on the earth.' So Elijah went to present himself to Ahab; and there was a severe famine in Samaria" (1 Kings 18:1–2).

Elijah had moments of greatness and moments of fear. When Queen Jezebel sought to end his life, Elijah ran and hid. He had this moment when he felt all alone, and in that moment, God did not come to Elijah in a powerful wind, a great earthquake, or a fire. God spoke to Elijah in a still, small voice. God met Elijah in his need not with His greatness but with His love. Elijah had such a close relationship with God through prayer, he was spoken about again in James 5:16–18.

> "Confess your trespasses to one another, and pray for one another, that you may be healed. The effective, fervent prayer of a righteous man avails much. Elijah was a man with a nature like ours, and he prayed

earnestly that it would not rain; and it did not rain on the land for three years and six months. And he prayed again, and the heaven gave rain, and the earth produced its fruit."

What is a fervent prayer? Fervent means passionate. A fervent prayer is a passionate prayer. Passion in your prayer life is developed because you earnestly and deeply care about the people and prayers. Strive toward passion and fervency in your prayers.

What about righteousness? Well, a righteous person is a person who has confessed his or her sins with a repentant heart. A person who humbles themselves before a mighty God, knowing that we cannot, but He can.

It is amazing to offer up prayers for others and see those prayers answered. Just look at the church when they offered up prayers for Peter while he was in prison.

"Peter was therefore kept in prison, but constant prayer was offered to God for him by the church. And when Herod was about to bring him out, that night Peter was sleeping, bound with two chains between two soldiers; and the guards before the door were keeping the prison. Now behold, an angel of the Lord stood by him, and a light shone in the prison; and he struck Peter on the side and raised him up, saying, "Arise quickly!" And his chains fell off his hands. Then the angel said to him, "Gird yourself and tie on your sandals"; and so he did. And he said to him, "Put on your garment and follow me." So he went out and followed him, and did not know that what was done by the angel was real, but thought he was seeing a vision. When they were past the first and the second guard posts, they came to the iron gate that leads to the city, which opened to them of its own accord; and they went out and went down one street, and immediately the angel departed from him.

And when Peter had come to himself, he said, "Now I know for certain that the Lord has sent His angel, and has delivered me from the hand of Herod and from all the expectation of the Jewish people." (Acts 12:5–11)

When you hear that there is power in a praying church, this is what that means. When God's people gather together in one accord, that means they come together in agreement, one heart, one mind, one decision. These church members stood steadfastly in their faith expecting God to answer their prayers. The church was in constant prayer for Peter. God is faithful to answer the prayers of those who love Him and are called according to His purpose. The angel appeared to Peter and led him to safety. Then Peter continued his work for the Lord.

Imagine if all these people had tried to fight their battles on their own. They would not have succeeded, but with prayer, God provided the victory. Only through Him can our prayer life be successful. That is why it is so important to establish a prayer life early in our Christian walk and to grow that prayer life as we walk our path with God.

There are so many times in my life that I have seen the power of prayer. As a church, we have prayed for others and witnessed the power of God working in that person's life. I have prayed individually and watched God move mountains in both my life and the lives of others. If you want to move mountains, pray in faith for the mountain to be moved. There is power in prayer. Always approach prayer with reverence, expecting to meet with God.

5

JOURNAL

A prayer journal is an important piece to our prayer life. Do you remember what you prayed for yesterday? How about last month? Writing down our prayers and being specific not only helps us to remember what to pray for when we go to God in prayer, but it is also a reminder of answered prayers.

While you do not have to use a prayer journal, if you will read through the book of Psalms in the Bible, they are written prayers set to music. The word psalm means a sacred song or hymn. David is credited with writing at least seventy-three psalms, and these were his thoughts and prayers journaled.

Probably one of the most recognized Psalm of David is Psalm 23:

"The Lord is my shepherd;
I shall not want.
He makes me to lie down in green pastures;
He leads me beside the still waters.
He restores my soul;
He leads me in the paths of righteousness for His name's sake.

Yea, though I walk through the valley of the shadow
of death,
I will fear no evil;
For You are with me;
Your rod and Your staff, they comfort me.
You prepare a table before me in the presence of my
enemies;
You anoint my head with oil;
My cup runs over.
Surely goodness and mercy shall follow me
All the days of my life;
And I will dwell in the house of the Lord
Forever." (Psalm 23:1–6)

I love reading through the book of Psalm. There is such praise to
our heavenly Father found in this book. These are prayers that are
still relevant today. Whether we are looking for worship, repentance,
cleansing, forgiveness, or restoration—you can find a Psalm related
to that.

Psalm 51 is a perfect example. This is a prayer that I have used
numerous times.

"Have mercy upon me, O God, according to Your
lovingkindness; According to the multitude of Your
tender mercies, blot out my transgressions. Wash me
thoroughly from my iniquity, and cleanse me from
my sin" (Psalm 51:1–2).

These scriptures are relevant to our walk with God. When I ask
God to set my soul on fire for Him, I use the verse "Restore to me the
joy of Your salvation" (Psalm 51:12). Remember that moment after
your salvation, that feeling that washed over you. That fire you felt to
tell others about Jesus. Wanting others to experience what you had
just experienced. That is the beauty of this verse.

This is why I stress a prayer journal. It allows you to recall these prayers later in life. I enjoy writing down my prayers for others. It helps me to formulate my thoughts, but I love to write. I also love to look back and see answered prayers. It is a way to remember who and what you are praying for. Writing out prayers like a Psalm to the Lord helps to express your thoughts and digs deeper into the specifics of your prayer.

If you do not know what to pray, start with writing out a prayer from Psalms that you identify with. Pick out a verse and tailor it to you. This helps make your prayer more personal while growing your prayer life. As you write out these prayers, it will become easier to express yourself in prayer.

Prayer used to feel very daunting to me. I was communicating with my Savior. Some days, I felt like I was babbling, not making much sense. There were days that I would walk away from a prayer feeling that I must be a disappointment to the Lord. Then someone bought me a prayer journal that contained scriptures from Daniel. I read about how he readied himself for prayer. Then, I found my quiet place, brought my Bible and journal, and readied myself to speak with my Lord. Such a difference in my prayer life.

I wrote daily in this journal, with a date next to each prayer. I felt so much closer to the Lord. There are still days where I am unsure what to pray, but now I know God knows my heart and I am not a disappointment. I now carry my journal with me wherever I go so I can write out my prayers at that moment.

In the Old Testament, they built altars to the Lord to remember answered prayers. If you read Genesis, you will see several instances when there was a personal encounter with the Lord, and an altar was built to remember this moment.

> "Abram passed through the land to the place of Shechem, as far as the terebinth tree of Moreh. And the Canaanites were then in the land.

> Then the Lord appeared to Abram and said, "To your descendants I will give this land." And there he built an altar to the Lord, who had appeared to him. And he moved from there to the mountain east of Bethel, and he pitched his tent with Bethel on the west and Ai on the east; there he built an altar to the Lord and called on the name of the Lord." (Genesis 12:6–8)

Each time a prayer is answered, mark it in some way in your journal. Maybe you date each prayer and then date the answer. You could just mark through it with a line or highlight it. Whatever is most comfortable for you. When you do this, you will have a permanent record of God's goodness, mercy, and love.

On the days you feel distant from God, or feel that He is not hearing your prayers, open a journal and comb through the pages of answers. I have walked through some faith-shaking difficult times, and no matter what is going on at that moment, I can see God's goodness, His grace, His mercy, and His understanding, and more through the pages of my prayer journals. They ground me in the knowledge that God is always present, working everything out for good. Even when I cannot see. Even when I do not know what to pray. God may not answer a prayer the way we think He should or in the timing we want, but He will always answer. Those answers are best for the life of the person we are praying for.

The world will try to bring you down. It will try to discourage you from serving the Lord. Remember this: no one can take away your record of answered prayers. They cannot take your journey with the Lord. Lean into the goodness of God. Reread your prayers. See God's hand in everything. Look at the blessings poured out in your life and the lives of those around you. There is no doubt that Jesus loves you. Refocus on that and keep walking with God.

I have several journals with names and dates of prayers. Some requests are longer than others. Some are one word, but all are important to me and God. I like to sit and look over these on occasion to be reminded of how God has moved in the lives of those around me. He is so gracious to listen to our intercessions on behalf of others. Prayer is such a personal experience. I feel when I pray that I have a direct line with God. In reality, I know that everyone has the same line to God that I do, but He listens to all of us as though we were the only one. What an amazing God we serve!

Prayer is between you and God.

> "Now in the morning, having risen a long while before daylight, He went out and departed to a solitary place; and there He prayed" (Mark 1:35).

There are so many different journals out there, you will have to find one that truly works for you. Some have scriptures on each page, some devotions; some are spiral-bound, and some have book spines. It really is a personal choice. If you do not want to buy a journal, just get a notepad or regular paper. There is nothing that says your prayers have to be written in a journal. You can write them on anything. The main point is to write them down. You can even type them up on the computer or write them on the back of receipts; just keep track of your prayers.

This is also beneficial when you get a request to pray for someone. Life is busy, and if we do not write it down, we tend to forget. Not that we do not have the desire to pray for others, but our minds run in a million different directions at once. Most of the time we will not remember that we forgot to pray for him or her until we see that person again or until it is mentioned at church. Then we carry around the guilt of having given our word that we would pray and forgot to do it. If we write it down, we will remember to lift up that request in prayer. Use the same method you use with the other prayers when this one is answered.

If possible, when someone asks you to pray for him or her, stop right then and pray. Whether it is over the phone or in person, you can pray together. If they are reaching out, they need prayer spoken over them at that moment. If you do not feel confident enough in your prayer life to pray out loud, then pray and ask God to give you the boldness to pray in front of others.

There is no perfect way to pray out loud. I have heard many different styles and variations. I have also heard the humbleness of a righteous prayer and felt a spirit-filled, place-shaking prayer. I have been so blessed by others when they pray out loud. Do not miss out on blessing someone else and yourself by not praying out loud in a group setting. Just pray from your heart and God will hear. Also, remember to write them down in your prayer journal so you can continue to lift their requests up in prayer.

A good example of intercessory prayer is found in Daniel's prayer for the people.

> "O Lord, according to all Your righteousness, I pray, let Your anger and Your fury be turned away from Your city Jerusalem, Your holy mountain; because for our sins, and for the iniquities of our fathers, Jerusalem and Your people are a reproach to all those around us. Now therefore, our God, hear the prayer of Your servant, and his supplications, and for the Lord's sake cause Your face to shine on Your sanctuary, which is desolate. O my God, incline Your ear and hear; open Your eyes and see our desolations, and the city which is called by Your name; for we do not present our supplications before You because of our righteous deeds, but because of Your great mercies. O Lord, hear! O Lord, forgive! O Lord, listen and act! Do not delay for Your own sake, my God, for Your city and Your people are called by Your name." (Daniel 9:16–19)

While Daniel is praying, Gabriel comes to tell Daniel that he is loved. God heard Daniel's prayer, his plea for his people.

Have you ever prayed for someone so earnestly that you felt the Spirit of God in your own life? God wants us to have a heart and compassion for others that we would intercede on their behalf. That we would desire the very best for their lives, just like Daniel did for his people.

If you want to be inspired, read Psalm 27. David expresses his fearless faith in this prayer to the Lord before being crowned king. He had boldness.

> "The Lord is my light and my salvation;
> Whom shall I fear? The Lord is the strength of my life;
> Of whom shall I be afraid?
> When the wicked came against me
> To eat up my flesh,
> My enemies and foes,
> They stumbled and fell.
> Though an army may encamp against me,
> My heart shall not fear;
> Though war may rise against me,
> In this I will be confident.
> One thing I have desired of the Lord,
> That will I seek:
> That I may dwell in the house of the Lord
> All the days of my life,
> To behold the beauty of the Lord,
> And to inquire in His temple.
> For in the time of trouble
> He shall hide me in His pavilion;
> In the secret place of His tabernacle
> He shall hide me; He shall set me high upon a rock.

And now my head shall be lifted up above my enemies
all around me;
Therefore I will offer sacrifices of joy in His tabernacle;
I will sing, yes, I will sing praises to the Lord.
Hear, O Lord, when I cry with my voice!
Have mercy also upon me, and answer me.
When You said, "Seek My face,"
My heart said to You, "Your face, Lord, I will seek."
Do not hide Your face from me;
Do not turn Your servant away in anger;
You have been my help;
Do not leave me nor forsake me,
O God of my salvation.
When my father and my mother forsake me,
Then the Lord will take care of me.
Teach me Your way, O Lord,
And lead me in a smooth path, because of my enemies.
Do not deliver me to the will of my adversaries;
For false witnesses have risen against me,
And such as breathe out violence.
I would have lost heart, unless I had believed
That I would see the goodness of the Lord
In the land of the living.
Wait on the Lord;
Be of good courage,
And He shall strengthen your heart;
Wait, I say, on the Lord!" (Psalm 27:1–14)

David was truly seeking the Lord through prayer. Although there are many mountaintop and valley experiences throughout the life of David, he always knew that prayer was his connection to God. He may have strayed from the Lord, but he returned to him in prayer. David's walk may have wavered, but his faith in the Lord stood firm.

Prayer truly changes everything. It is such an important part of our Christian life. Walk into this life knowing that you have a personal connection to your Savior. He wants to hear from you on a regular basis. A prayer journal is an excellent way to keep your prayer life on track and to see growth in your prayers.

6

DIFFERENT

When you accept salvation, you are changed. The old life is gone and you have this new life. You actually want to be more like Jesus each day.

We cannot go back to living like we were, nor do we want to. We have a desire to walk a different path. You may be saying that there is nothing wrong with who you are right now. You might be right. However, to complete God's plan for your life, you will have to grow and be moldable so that you can be the person God knows you can be.

After receiving the free gift of salvation, we are called to spread the love of Jesus to the world so others might attain the same gift. We cannot do that if we look like the world. No one is going to want what we have if we look like they do. That does not give them any hope that life could be any better than it is currently. When you are living in despair and you see someone who has peace, you want that same peace. If the people around you are all in despair, then they have nothing to offer you for a better life, a hope for the future.

Jesus gives us the Great Commission in Matthew.

"And Jesus came and spoke to them, saying, "All authority has been given to Me in heaven and on earth. Go therefore and make disciples of all the nations, baptizing them in the name of the Father and of the Son and of the Holy Spirit, teaching them to observe all things that I have commanded you; and lo, I am with you always, even to the end of the age." Amen." (Matthew 28:18–20)

Go and tell others about Jesus. Being different is hard because you may be the only one trying to be different. Your family may not have salvation, your friends may not have salvation, and you are trying to live a life for God without the support of other Christians. It is hard to live a different life when those around you do not. You will see a difference between you and them. Unfortunately, some may not choose to stay around. That is the sad part about this. I still love all my family and friends, but some choose to stay away because I am a Christian. It all has to do with the conviction they feel by being around you. It has nothing to do with what you say or do not say. The best thing you can do for them is put them in your prayer journal and lift them up to God in prayer. He is the changer of hearts. He can make a difference in their lives just like He did for you.

Remember that no matter where you are, whether at work or out with friends, in church, or at home, it is always best to do the right thing. Not the OK thing or the fair thing, but what is right in the eyes of the Lord. This may not be the course of action that the world would take, and it might mean you have to take a stand at work, but we cannot compromise our beliefs just to make someone else happy. That is not what Jesus would do. Even when it was unpopular. Even when people stood against Him, Jesus still stood for what is right and just. He even called out the unjust. He referred to the religious leaders of the time as a brood of vipers. That was unheard of to go against the leaders of the church. That was exactly what they needed to hear because each one of those leaders was in need of a Savior. They just did not realize it. There was no mistaking it after what Jesus said.

> "But woe to you, scribes and Pharisees, hypocrites! For you shut up the kingdom of heaven against men; for you neither go in yourselves, nor do you allow those who are entering to go in. Woe to you, scribes and Pharisees, hypocrites! For you devour widows' houses, and for a pretense make long prayers. Therefore you will receive greater condemnation." (Matthew 23:13–14)

> "Therefore you are witnesses against yourselves that you are sons of those who murdered the prophets. Fill up, then, the measure of your fathers' guilt. Serpents, brood of vipers! How can you escape the condemnation of hell? Therefore, indeed, I send you prophets, wise men, and scribes: some of them you will kill and crucify, and some of them you will scourge in your synagogues and persecute from city to city, that on you may come all the righteous blood shed on the earth, from the blood of righteous Abel to the blood of Zechariah, son of Berechiah, whom you murdered between the temple and the altar. Assuredly, I say to you, all these things will come upon this generation." (Matthew 23:31–36)

You are the only Jesus some people will ever see. They may never make it into a church house, but they are still out there searching for the salvation you have. They will look to you to see if your life is any different from theirs. If you look like the world and conform to the world, how can your light shine and show people that a life with Jesus is the best life? You may never fully realize how many lives you will touch by simply living different from the world.

I remember a story I heard as a child about a family who watched their neighbor every week pull out of the driveway and go to church. That family saw that the neighbor was faithful, and one day, they too got up and went to the church. They told the story to the pastor about how the neighbor's faithfulness is what brought them there. I have never forgotten that story, and each time I pull out of my driveway, I pray for my neighbors. Such a small act of obedience can make such a big difference.

> And do not be conformed to this world, but be transformed by the renewing of your mind, that you may prove what is that good and acceptable and perfect will of God. For I say, through the grace given to me, to everyone who is among you, not to think of himself more highly than he ought to think, but to think soberly, as God has dealt to each one a measure of faith. (Romans 12:2–3)

He knows everything I have done. He knows my past mistakes. He knows my current mishaps. He loves me even when I feel that I am unlovable. Being loved by the Lord makes me want to be a better person. I want to be different. I want to walk with Him every day. I want to be the best version of myself. I cannot thank Him enough for everything He has done for me. I have hope for the future. I look at the world differently. I am completely loved. He loves you too and wants a relationship with you. He wants to shine through your life.

People will be able to see the love of Jesus in you. I have had many instances where I did not have to say a word, but people knew I was a Christian. It is such a compliment when that happens because I know I am doing something to show the love of Jesus to others. You may never know the impact that you have on another person's life. They may be watching you and never say a word. Just because you do not get feedback from others does not mean the light of God in your life is not shining brightly. You can say so much by doing what is right in the face of adversity without ever having to say a word. You can show love to others even when love is not shown back. You can extend grace and mercy when you do not receive them in return. You can be a light pointing the way to a life of love with Jesus Christ. Do not be like the world. Be different.

An example of a life changed is Paul. Paul had a heart for service. While everyone saw Paul for what he was doing, God saw Paul's heart. Paul worked for the Lord, not with the Lord. Paul was spiritually blind. He was physically blinded on the Damascus Road. While he could not see, Paul had to completely trust the Lord with his life. His eyes were spiritually opened. From that point forward, Paul worked with the Lord. His service now had meaning.

All the people who had heard or seen Paul's persecution of the church could have discounted Paul and chosen not to listen to his preaching. The disciples could have chosen not to welcome him in because of what they knew about his past. That was not the case; Paul was immediately welcomed. They even referred to him as brother. The disciples trusted the Lord, and they could see the change in Paul's life. Paul's past was just that—in the past. The disciples accepted Paul for the person he was. Christians accepted Paul for the servant he was, not the person he used to be.

Paul encountered many people who knew him before and questioned his service to the Lord, and each time he told his story about how God changed his life. Paul told them about the love of Jesus. Even King Agrippa said Paul had almost persuaded him to become a Christian. Paul's goals changed from persecuting Christians to converting people to Christianity. The Damascus Road conversion changed the course of Paul's life. He became a new creation. He started walking the road with the Lord. He was different.

7

HUMBLE

This one might sting a little. We cannot serve two masters. We cannot serve self and God. Humbleness, God can use. Pride … God cannot use. If we want to grow closer to God and for our relationship to flourish, we have to realize that everything we have had, currently have, or will have in the future is because of God. He gives and He takes away. He alone sustains us, not we ourselves. As humans, we like to make accomplishments in our lives. We like recognition. Pride gets in the way of our service because we start to think we can manage this life on our own. I used to think I would take care of all the small stuff in my life and only ask God for help with the big stuff, and somehow He would be so proud of me for handling my own life. I could not have been more wrong. God wants to be in every part of our lives, the small, the big, the enormous, the everyday things we take for granted—He is in those too.

> "No one can serve two masters; for either he will hate the one and love the other, or else he will be loyal to the one and despise the other. You cannot serve God and mammon.

"Therefore I say to you, do not worry about your life, what you will eat or what you will drink; nor about your body, what you will put on. Is not life more than food and the body more than clothing? Look at the birds of the air, for they neither sow nor reap nor gather into barns; yet your heavenly Father feeds them. Are you not of more value than they? Which of you by worrying can add one cubit to his stature?" (Matthew 6:24–27)

"Pride goes before destruction, and a haughty spirit before a fall. Better to be of a humble spirit with the lowly, than to divide the spoil with the proud" (Proverbs 16:18–19).

Have you ever thought about that? God does not need your pride. Pride believes you have everything you need to live this life on your own. Pride does not need help from anyone or anything to accomplish goals and tasks. Whatever we do in this life, we have to remember that if we boast, we boast in what God has done and what He will do. It is better to acknowledge our need for God's guidance than to think we can live this life on our own, apart from God.

How do we achieve humbleness? First, we need to recognize that apart from Him, we can do nothing. That is right. He is the reason you woke up this morning. That puts things in perspective. Every morning, I thank God for giving me another day on this earth to make a difference for Him. Second, we need to know that everything good in our lives is because of Him. We have food to eat, a roof over our heads, and clothes on our backs. Be thankful. All that may not be exactly what you want, but you have it. That is what matters. All the rest of it—size, brand, color, etc.—are just details that do not matter to the Kingdom of God.

"I am the true vine, and My Father is the vinedresser. Every branch in Me that does not bear fruit He takes away; and every branch that bears fruit He prunes, that it may bear more fruit. You are already clean because of the word which I have spoken to you. Abide in Me, and I in you. As the branch cannot bear fruit of itself, unless it abides in the vine, neither can you, unless you abide in Me.

> "I am the vine, you are the branches. He who abides in Me, and I in him, bears much fruit; for without Me you can do nothing. If anyone does not abide in Me, he is cast out as a branch and is withered; and they gather them and throw them into the fire, and they are burned. If you abide in Me, and My words abide in you, you will ask what you desire, and it shall be done for you. By this My Father is glorified, that you bear much fruit; so you will be My disciples." (John 15:1–8)

We can spend our whole lives trying to achieve status, house, car, and clothes, and when we pass from this life and are face to face with Jesus, will any of that stuff matter to Him. What will He say when you meet Him? My life goal is to hear, "Well done, my good and faithful servant."

What is your goal? Have you ever thought about it? Take some time and think about what you want out of this life. Because while eternity lasts forever, but we are only on this earth for a short time. You only get one chance at this life. Yesterday is gone and cannot be redone. Today is the day to start over. Make every second count.

The true character of humbleness can be found in Luke 7.

> "Then one of the Pharisees asked Him to eat with him. And He went to the Pharisee's house, and sat down to eat. And behold, a woman in the city who was a sinner, when she knew that Jesus sat at the table in the Pharisee's house, brought an alabaster flask of fragrant oil, and stood at His feet behind Him weeping; and

she began to wash His feet with her tears, and wiped them with the hair of her head; and she kissed His feet and anointed them with the fragrant oil. Now when the Pharisee who had invited Him saw this, he spoke to himself, saying, "This Man, if He were a prophet, would know who and what manner of woman this is who is touching Him, for she is a sinner."

And Jesus answered and said to him, "Simon, I have something to say to you."

So he said, "Teacher, say it."

"There was a certain creditor who had two debtors. One owed five hundred denarii, and the other fifty. And when they had nothing with which to repay, he freely forgave them both. Tell Me, therefore, which of them will love him more?"

Simon answered and said, "I suppose the one whom he forgave more."

And He said to him, "You have rightly judged." Then He turned to the woman and said to Simon, "Do you see this woman? I entered your house; you gave Me no water for My feet, but she has washed My feet with her tears and wiped them with the hair of her head. You gave Me no kiss, but this woman has not ceased to kiss My feet since the time I came in. You did not anoint My head with oil, but this woman has anointed My feet with fragrant oil. Therefore I say to you, her sins, which are many, are forgiven, for she loved much. But to whom little is forgiven, the same loves little."

Then He said to her, "Your sins are forgiven."

And those who sat at the table with Him began to say to themselves, "Who is this who even forgives sins?"

> Then He said to the woman, "Your faith has saved
> you. Go in peace." (Luke 7:36–50)

That is humbleness. This woman recognized the sovereignty of who God is and that she was in need of a Savior. She recognized that she did not deserve forgiveness, so she honored Him by giving all she had in the bottle of perfume and washing His feet. She showed not only her love for Jesus but a true servant's heart.

The Pharisee could not see past his religion and status to see his need for a Savior. He was too caught up in religious acts and titles to worry about actual service. The Pharisee immediately looked at what he could see about the woman. All he could see was her sins. Jesus saw the woman's heart.

Have you ever washed someone else's feet? It is a humbling experience to serve someone else. To really look at others with your heart. We see past what is going on in the world and what is going on in our lives and stop for a moment to honor someone else.

I think about my Savior when He went to the cross. When He was beaten at the post. The pain He endured. He never said a word. Jesus was accused and never defended Himself. He was sentenced and He never gave a defense. Not because He was guilty but because His sacrifice was the only way. Jesus chose to die for me. Jesus chose to die for every person, past, present, and future to have the opportunity to spend eternity in heaven with Him. He loves us enough to be marred more than any man. He loves us enough to be nailed to a cross. He loves us enough to take on the sin of the world. What was going through His mind when all of this was happening? Jesus said it perfectly when He asked the Father to forgive them. He was on that cross thinking about you and me. That is truly humbling. In His time of need, He was thinking of me. He was and is loving every person in the world.

Walking with God is an active relationship that requires both parties. We cannot always take from God and never give. That type of relationship never works. You have to give—your time, your talents, your heart, your service. He desires to have a relationship with you, but you have to desire a relationship with Him. Relationships are built on humbleness, not pride.

Your relationship with God takes work. There is nothing in this life that does not require you to put forth an effort. A relationship with God works the same way. You will get out of it what you put into it. You want to have a close walk with God. To feel the fullness and love that only comes from God. You have to make time every day to spend with your heavenly Father. God wants to work through you. You have to be a willing servant. You have to turn your life over to God. Step back and allow His leadership in your life. That takes humbleness to know you cannot walk through this life alone. Know that God can do all things through you. Then allow Him to do it. Keep that relationship close and see the difference it makes in your life.

I could not do any of the things God has called me to do without Him by my side. Apart from the Lord, I am nothing. Only with Him can I achieve the plans He has for me. It has been amazing and humbling to see God at work in my life. No, this is not my plan. It is much better than anything I could have planned. I am in awe of the Lord that He would choose a sinner like me for His service. No matter how busy I am, I will always feel that there is more that I could be doing. I will serve my Savior until the whole world hears about the love of Jesus Christ.

8

PATHWAY

We each have a path to walk with God. This is the direction in which He wants our lives to go. He has plans for you that, most likely, are something you have never thought you would be doing. It is up to us if we allow Him to have that control over our lives and lead us in His ways and not our own. I remember when I was younger and had all these plans for my life when I got older. Nothing on that list worked out for me.

By nature I am a planner, so relinquishing control is not something that comes easily. I used to schedule everything. My phone was so full of appointments, meetings, events, and such that I did not see where there was time to do anything else.

But God never gave up on me. He nudged and convicted and pulled until I finally saw why His path is so important. My light was not shining at all for God. I was living my own way. I called myself a Christian, but I was not truly committed to serving Christ. Once I gave my life fully to God, He worked a miracle. My life is still super busy, but I have all this extra time I did not know existed, to serve God. I give God all the glory and thank Him for never giving up on me. He truly is a light to my path.

"Your word is a lamp to my feet and a light to my path" (Psalm 119:105).

You can walk with God. I will never say this step is easy, but it is so worth it. This is a step of obedience to the call that God has placed on your life. You do not have to know what that is, just trust in Him and allow Him to lead and guide you. You do not have to know where you are going, He knows and He wants the very best for your life. He loves you more than you can ever love yourself so you know that His pathway is going to be the best.

"A man's heart plans his way, but the Lord directs his steps" (Proverbs 16:9).

Now, when you step on that pathway, get ready. The evil one does not want you serving God, following God, or growing in your faith. Here come the stumbling blocks. He is going to try to get you to back off of the pathway and sit down. While you sit, he is winning. If you do not fully commit to the Lord, the evil one wins. When you stop serving and following God, the evil one wins. These are small victories, but he will take what he can get. It is his ultimate desire to ruin your witness for God. I have seen people let the evil one in, and it destroyed their walk with God. I have seen Christians who look just like the world—they have no fruit to show that they are a Christian, just a title that they wear. How heartbreakingly sad. My heart hurts for those who have never known the fullness that comes from walking with God.

Walking the path with God means you are doing His will for your life. There truly is nothing greater than the work you do for the Lord. Nothing will be more fulfilling than a close relationship with God. We do not walk by sight, because with our sight, we cannot see what is ahead of us, we just see all the roadblocks in our way. When we focus on our faith, the roadblocks disappear and we walk ahead, not needing to see the future because we know God does. He guides our steps and that is enough.

One example of God directing someone's pathway is found in Acts.

> "Now a certain woman named Lydia heard us. She was a seller of purple from the city of Thyatira, who worshiped God. The Lord opened her heart to heed the things spoken by Paul. And when she and her household were baptized, she begged us, saying, "If you have judged me to be faithful to the Lord, come to my house and stay." So she persuaded us." (Acts 16:14–15)

Lydia was a successful businesswoman. The Bible says she was a seller of purple. Purple was something that was worn by the wealthy. From this, you can see that Lydia worked hard to make a name for herself and through that developed a lucrative business. One day, she was going to the riverside for prayer and God opened her heart. After Lydia accepted salvation, her heart was on fire for the Lord and she tells her whole family. She wanted her family to have the same thing that she just experienced. They all accepted salvation and were baptized. Immediately, Lydia stepped on her pathway by inviting Paul and Silas to her home. She had a heart for hospitality and started her service to the Lord.

Lydia could have gone back to her life. She could have determined that she was already so busy making a life for herself that she did not have time to serve the Lord. Instead, she made time for the Lord. She put her service as a priority in her life. We see later in Acts after Paul and Silas are released from prison that they come to Lydia's house and visit with the brethren. Through this, we see that Lydia has opened her home to church meetings. She is continuing her walk with the Lord and saying yes to serving Him.

Lydia's life shows us that we can have a career, family, and service. That we are not too busy to walk the pathway that the Lord has laid before us. This pathway is ours and ours alone to walk. God has it planned out. He just asks you to join Him on this journey. If Lydia's life is any example, she discovered how rewarding service to the Lord can be. Our lives are so much more when we walk with the Lord.

Another example is the life of Simon Peter, who was a fisherman. This was how he made his living and supported his family. Then Peter and his brother, Andrew, met Jesus. They put down their nets and followed Jesus. Peter left everything he knew to walk with Jesus. He was Jesus's first disciple. Jesus did not choose him because of his degrees on the wall or his years of study. Jesus saw Peter's heart. Peter was the first to say that Jesus was the Son of God. Peter walked way outside his comfort zone. He grew in his faith and boldness. He had conviction in his beliefs. He was humbled in his service. Peter emerged as a leader. The name Peter means rock, which is what Jesus said He would build his church on. None of this would have been possible had Peter not taken that first step onto the path when Jesus called him to follow.

You will never fully know the depth, the reach, the impact that living your life for the Lord will have on others. To you, it is simply one step on a pathway, one extremely personal relationship that called you to action. Just a simple, humbling act of service for the One who gave everything for you. Maybe it was a small interaction to you, but to those searching and longing, it could make a huge impression.

Think of it this way. One day someone will tell your story. That person will tell of how what you did made a difference in his or her life. How he or she could see Jesus through you and that the love of Jesus made a difference in their life. And this person will go on to tell of walking with Jesus.

However small the interaction may be, you made a difference. You made the world a better place for that one person, all because you made the choice to take that step and walk the pathway that the Lord lay before you.

9

STEPPING OUT
FOR GOD

Here is where you have to make an important decision. Are you going to do what God has called you to do? Are you going to take that step? Look through your Bible at the heroes of faith. Did they ever stay in the same place? Were they ever comfortable and content? Did they serve God from the comfort of their home? The answer to all these questions is no. God called them out, sometimes to move, live in a cave, leave their homeland, travel great distances—all in the name of service.

One of the great calls to step outside her comfort zone was Mary. Mary was called to be Jesus's Mother. She did not know the magnitude of her decision, but she was faithful. In her time, Mary could have been stoned to death for what God called her to do. We find her story in Luke.

> "Now in the sixth month the angel Gabriel was sent by God to a city of Galilee named Nazareth, to a virgin betrothed to a man whose name was Joseph, of the

house of David. The virgin's name was Mary. And having come in, the angel said to her, "Rejoice, highly favored one, the Lord is with you; blessed are you among women!"

But when she saw him, she was troubled at his saying, and considered what manner of greeting this was. Then the angel said to her, "Do not be afraid, Mary, for you have found favor with God. And behold, you will conceive in your womb and bring forth a Son, and shall call His name Jesus. He will be great, and will be called the Son of the Highest; and the Lord God will give Him the throne of His father David. And He will reign over the house of Jacob forever, and of His kingdom there will be no end."

Then Mary said to the angel, "How can this be, since I do not know a man?"

And the angel answered and said to her, "The Holy Spirit will come upon you, and the power of the Highest will overshadow you; therefore, also, that Holy One who is to be born will be called the Son of God. Now indeed, Elizabeth your relative has also conceived a son in her old age; and this is now the sixth month for her who was called barren. For with God nothing will be impossible."

Then Mary said, "Behold the maidservant of the Lord! Let it be to me according to your word." And the angel departed from her." (Luke 1:26–38)

What if she had told the angel no? How different our world would be. Instead, she says, "Let it be to me according to Your Word." She probably had no idea how she was going to explain this to Joseph or her family. Her friends would not have understood either. This was not a regular occurrence. She had no one to talk with about what was fixing to happen. Still, we see further in scripture that Mary rejoiced in her work for the Lord. Luke 1:46 starts with Mary's song.

> "And Mary said:
> "'My soul magnifies the Lord,
> And my spirit has rejoiced in God my Savior.
> For He has regarded the lowly state of His maidservant;
> For behold, henceforth all generations will call me blessed.
> For He who is mighty has done great things for me,
> And holy is His name.
> And His mercy is on those who fear Him
> From generation to generation.
> He has shown strength with His arm;
> He has scattered the proud in the imagination of their hearts.
> He has put down the mighty from their thrones,
> And exalted the lowly.
> He has filled the hungry with good things,
> And the rich He has sent away empty.
> He has helped His servant Israel,
> In remembrance of His mercy,
> As He spoke to our fathers,
> To Abraham and to his seed forever.'" (Luke 1:46–55)

Mary has no idea where this first step would lead. She took the step anyway. There were so many twists and turns on this road, including a life that she and Joseph would not have imagined for themselves. Each time the Lord told them to step, they stepped. When the Lord appeared to Joseph and told him to go to Egypt, they went. This was not a place that Mary and Joseph had talked about living or was part of their five-year plan. It was where God told them to go. What a beautiful life of service.

We get so comfortable with our routines that we do not want to venture outside our comfort zone to work for God. God has sent me to some really uncomfortable places. Most of the time I have no idea what I am doing there, I just know I am supposed to be there. This one is not easy. It is easy to keep the same routine—to do the same things every day. To coast through life. It is hard to be completely outside what is comfortable and familiar and to work toward what God wants you to accomplish through this experience. Some days the steps will not make sense. You will not understand the big picture. I have been there.

By nature, we are creatures of habit. We really do not like change. We buy the same brands, watch the same shows, associate with the same people, and maybe even drive the same way to work every day.

But change is inevitable. They quit making your favorite brand of cookies. The road you normally take to work is closed; your job moves you to a new city. We are not the same people we were a year ago. Change is going to happen. It is up to us whether we allow that change to include God. Are you ready to take that first step?

You look at one step and think there is no possible way that God is in this step. This step is just one in a larger plan. He has already gone before you. He has made the way. He just wants your trust and dedication to see this plan through to the end. That is the commitment to Him. Before you take that step, pray that whatever His will is, it will be accomplished. That changes your perspective. You are now in for the long haul—to see this to its completion.

Each step, although small in your mind, is significant in the plan. Do not jump ahead. If you miss a step, the whole plan is off course. What I mean by that is that God prepares us prior, during, and after the step. He continually molds you, and if you miss the moldable opportunity, you may not be prepared for the next step. Each step is vital in our walk with God. We move when He moves. We wait upon the Lord and are patient.

Patience is not something that I have an abundance of. God

has worked on me and molded me in this area. I am still a work in progress. If you have an area where you struggle, God is there to help you as well. If you allow Him, He will mold you in this area and all areas of your life. Look for the moldable opportunities and allow them to strengthen your walk with the Lord.

We see what is right in front of our faces. God is the entire picture. He knows the road ahead. He sees every mountaintop and every valley. We are shortsighted. We just see what is currently going on around us. This step we are in is what we see. We have no way to know how this situation will work out or what will happen next. It is easy to allow the current surroundings to distract us from the walk ahead. There are times that we cannot see how this will possibly work out, but if we keep walking, the road ahead will become clear when the time is right. The Lord knows when you are ready for the next step.

It is hard not to move when you see things going wrong. The natural reaction is to get out of that situation. That may not be God's plan. I have walked through situations that were crumbling around me, praying every step of the way, not knowing the plan or the purpose but knowing God said to stay on course. I can look back now and see the growth and changes that were made in me because of the situations I walked through. Each had a purpose and made me the person I am today. With God by my side, even the bad days are not so bad. He makes everything better and brighter just knowing He has a plan for my life and that He loves me enough that He has worked out every detail of that plan.

Remember that with each step you take, the word of the Lord goes out and does not return void.

> "For as the rain comes down, and the snow from heaven, and do not return there, but water the earth, and make it bring forth and bud, that it may give seed to the sower and bread to the eater, so shall My word

be that goes forth from My mouth; it shall not return to Me void, but it shall accomplish what I please, and it shall prosper in the thing for which I sent it." (Isaiah 55:10–11)

"But be doers of the word, and not hearers only, deceiving yourselves. For if anyone is a hearer of the word and not a doer, he is like a man observing his natural face in a mirror; for he observes himself, goes away, and immediately forgets what kind of man he was. But he who looks into the perfect law of liberty and continues in it, and is not a forgetful hearer but a doer of the work, this one will be blessed in what he does." (James 1:22–25)

Be a doer of the Word. That is your first call in your Christian life, to tell others about Jesus. When you take that step, the next step comes easier and eventually you realize that every step you take is for God.

There is something so powerful yet so wonderful about the name of Jesus. When you talk to others about Jesus, you feel this fullness inside, a fullness that can only come from the Lord. A feeling to give you the reassurance that you are not alone. This conversation is not just between you and them. The Spirit is there and will guide you, if you allow Him. Such a simple task, mentioning the name of Jesus, can lead to powerful conversations. Open your heart to His guidance and His leadership. One step at a time.

10

GUIDANCE

I would be lost without the guidance I receive from the Holy Spirit. As Christians, we have an amazing resource that we rarely tap in to. The Holy Spirit comes to live inside us when we accept salvation. We do not get just a small part of the Holy Spirit; we receive the entire Holy Spirit. It is up to us how much we access. The Holy Spirit is the third person of the Trinity.

We seek guidance from so many places. We check our daily horoscope, we look to advice columns, we seek out counsel, we ask friends and family, and the list goes on. The One who can give true guidance is usually the last one we ask. His guidance is perfect every time. His ways are better than anything we could get from man. So why do we not seek Him out first? Mostly, I believe it is because we are comfortable. We like our current life situation, and if we ask for guidance from the Lord, we may have to change that situation.

Psalm 118:8 says it perfectly: "It is better to trust in the Lord than to put confidence in man."

God's guidance is best.

I have experienced so many times where God's guidance was to do something completely outside my comfort zone. One of the hardest was moving churches. I was so comfortable at my church. I knew all the people. I was used to the weekly routine. But I knew something was missing. Still, I dug in and did not want to leave. Looking back now, I can see the growth each time God called me to move. I am thankful for each church family for being part of my journey. Each one holds a special place in my heart. If I had not followed God's guidance, then I would not be the person that I am today. I am thankful He never gave up on me and that He kept working on me to move.

Guidance means different things to different people. Some look at guidance as the one you go to for advice. Some look at guidance as the one you look to when things go wrong. Although neither of these ways is wrong, something is missing: that everyday guidance when you need to make decisions. The every-step guidance when you do not see the bigger picture. The every-moment guidance when we are one instant from talking to someone about Jesus. God wants to guide us every moment of every day. It is up to us to allow that.

Where would Joshua have been if he had not followed the guidance from the Lord? The walls of Jericho would have been a lot harder to breach. The Word of the Lord came to Joshua, telling him exactly what do to in this battle. We see his exact instructions in Joshua 6.

> "Now Jericho was securely shut up because of the children of Israel; none went out, and none came in. And the Lord said to Joshua: "See! I have given Jericho into your hand, its king, and the mighty men of valor. You shall march around the city, all you men of war; you shall go all around the city once. This you shall do six days. And seven priests shall bear seven trumpets of rams' horns before the ark. But the seventh day you shall march around the city seven times, and the priests shall blow the trumpets. It shall come to pass, when they make a long blast with the ram's horn, and

when you hear the sound of the trumpet, that all the people shall shout with a great shout; then the wall of the city will fall down flat. And the people shall go up every man straight before him." (Joshua 6:1–5)

I can see Joshua listening intently to these instructions. He has the faith that God will do what He says He will. He could have told the Lord that people will look at him, point, and make fun of him for marching around the city. He could have said no. Joshua was a faithful servant of God. He was in this situation because he had followed the guidance of the Lord. Let us catch up with Joshua and see his reaction to this guidance.

> "Then Joshua the son of Nun called the priests and said to them, "Take up the ark of the covenant, and let seven priests bear seven trumpets of rams' horns before the ark of the Lord." And he said to the people, "Proceed, and march around the city, and let him who is armed advance before the ark of the Lord."
>
> So it was, when Joshua had spoken to the people, that the seven priests bearing the seven trumpets of rams' horns before the Lord advanced and blew the trumpets, and the ark of the covenant of the Lord followed them. The armed men went before the priests who blew the trumpets, and the rear guard came after the ark, while the priests continued blowing the trumpets. Now Joshua had commanded the people, saying, "You shall not shout or make any noise with your voice, nor shall a word proceed out of your mouth, until the day I say to you, 'Shout!' Then you shall shout." So he had the ark of the Lord circle the city, going around it once. Then they came into the camp and lodged in the camp.

And Joshua rose early in the morning, and the priests took up the ark of the Lord. Then seven priests bearing seven trumpets of rams' horns before the ark of the Lord went on continually and blew with the trumpets. And the armed men went before them. But the rear guard came after the ark of the Lord, while the priests continued blowing the trumpets. And the second day they marched around the city once and returned to the camp. So they did six days." (Joshua 6:6–14)

So Joshua went straight and told his people about God's plan. There was no questioning or second thoughts. There was no deal-making with God about what Joshua was willing to do. The people of God obeyed. They did not question Joshua or say that they had to hear it from God before they would obey. They knew that Joshua was a man of God, that God had spoken with Joshua, and that God would not lead them astray. They followed God's guidance. And they did this for six days. Talk about patience! We do not like to wait in line for five minutes to get food, much less camped out for six days to overtake a city. I imagine this was such an interesting sight, God's people working together. What happened on the seventh day?

"But it came to pass on the seventh day that they rose early, about the dawning of the day, and marched around the city seven times in the same manner. On that day only they marched around the city seven times. And the seventh time it happened, when the priests blew the trumpets, that Joshua said to the people: "Shout, for the Lord has given you the city! Now the city shall be doomed by the Lord to destruction, it and all who are in it. Only Rahab the harlot shall live, she and all who are with her in the house, because she hid the messengers that we sent. And you, by all means abstain from the accursed things, lest you become accursed when you take of the accursed things, and make the camp of Israel a curse, and trouble it. But all the silver and gold, and vessels of bronze and iron, are consecrated to the Lord; they shall come into the treasury of the Lord."

So the people shouted when the priests blew the trumpets. And it happened when the people heard the sound of the trumpet, and the people shouted with a great shout, that the wall fell down flat. Then the people went up into the city, every man straight before him, and they took the city. And they utterly destroyed all that was in the city, both man and woman, young and old, ox and sheep and donkey, with the edge of the sword.

But Joshua had said to the two men who had spied out the country, "Go into the harlot's house, and from there bring out the woman and all that she has, as you swore to her." And the young men who had been spies went in and brought out Rahab, her father, her mother, her brothers, and all that she had. So they brought out all her relatives and left them outside the camp of Israel. But they burned the city and all that was in it with fire. Only the silver and gold, and the vessels of bronze and iron, they put into the treasury of the house of the Lord. And Joshua spared Rahab the harlot, her father's household, and all that she had. So she dwells in Israel to this day, because she hid the messengers whom Joshua sent to spy out Jericho.

Then Joshua charged them at that time, saying, "Cursed be the man before the Lord who rises up and builds this city Jericho; he shall lay its foundation

with his firstborn, and with his youngest he shall set
up its gates."

So the Lord was with Joshua, and his fame spread
throughout all the country." (Joshua 6:15–27)

It happened just as the Lord told Joshua it would. The walls of
Jericho fell and Joshua did as the Lord commanded. He followed
through. What a great example of what God can do through us if
we are willing to follow Him. This was not only a testament to the
men following Joshua but to everyone who inhabited Jericho. They
got a chance to see the power of God working for seven days. They
had a chance to change, but Rahab was the only person who took
that opportunity. She was spared from the battle along with her
household. Rahab started over, living a life for God. We see later that
Rahab is part of King David's lineage, all because of her decision to
follow the Lord. What a difference the Lord can make in our lives too.

Walking through this life is tough. Each day we are faced with
obstacles, forks in the road, stumbling blocks. Walking alone is so
frustrating. You know the feeling. When you get home from work
and you cannot even talk about your day because of the level of
frustration you feel. Your whole demeanor toward your family has
changed. They do not even want to be around you. You carry all this
anger and frustration with you, like baggage, everywhere you go.
With God's guidance, you can put that baggage down. It does not
change your circumstances; it changes you. And that is the point—
to be a better version of yourself. For you to be better when you are
around your family so those relationships do not suffer because of
your day.

If you walk with God and follow His guidance, then eventually,
your circumstances change too. The people at work see a different
you—one who takes everything that is piled on and still works for
the glory of the Lord. One of two things will happen. They will either
want what you have or despise you for your peace. If it is the latter,

you know it is time to wipe your feet off at the door and move on. Put them on your prayer list because God is the changer of hearts.

> "And when you go into a household, greet it. If the household is worthy, let your peace come upon it. But if it is not worthy, let your peace return to you. And whoever will not receive you nor hear your words, when you depart from that house or city, shake off the dust from your feet. Assuredly, I say to you, it will be more tolerable for the land of Sodom and Gomorrah in the day of judgment than for that city!" (Matthew 10:12–15)

I walked away from a job that I loved because of people. I sought God's guidance, and He let me know it was time to move on. It was not easy. Starting over never is, but if it is God's plan, it is always the right plan. After I left, I had to let go and turn it all over to God. To be the person God wants me to be means I have to forgive and let go. That means everything I went through, all of it, needed to go into bags. I had to set this baggage down and not pick it up again. Of course I am talking figuratively, but you can be literal about it. Take everything that reminds you of what you went through or the person you were and put it in a box or bag. Close it up, zip it up, and put it away or throw it away. Those things are not you anymore. You are a child of God. You are following His ways and His guidance for your life.

People are not going to understand the decisions you make, and that is OK. Do not worry about making decisions that please the world. You will even find that many people who claim to be Christians will question your decisions and the plan God has for your life. Again, do not worry about them. They do not have to understand your relationship with God. Just because we all use the label Christian does not mean that we all think the same.

I have been questioned many times about my walk with God. My walk with God is mine alone and is not for others to understand unless I choose to share. That is why it is called a personal relationship. The way God communicates with me and what He has called me to do will not be the same as your experience. That is the way it is supposed to be. Do not let the things people say to you derail you from the plan God has laid out for your life. What God thinks about the plan is the only thing that is important. He alone is the One to look to and follow. We do not follow people, so their opinions essentially do not matter.

You are in good company. The world did not understand Jesus either. He came to do the will of His Father that sent Him. No matter the cost, Jesus accomplished that will.

> "He came to His own, and His own did not receive Him. But as many as received Him, to them He gave the right to become children of God, to those who believe in His name" (John 1:11–12).

> "And He was withdrawn from them about a stone's throw, and He knelt down and prayed, saying, "Father, if it is Your will, take this cup away from Me; nevertheless not My will, but Yours, be done" (Luke 22:41–42).

Jesus knew what He was fixing to go through on the cross. The pain and the anguish He was going to endure. His prayer is so humbled—not My will, but Yours be done. When is the last time you prayed that prayer? Father, not my will, but Yours be done. Jesus is our example of how to live, and if He can do the Father's will, what is holding us back?

11

LEADERSHIP

Leadership is such an interesting word. Leadership is the responsibility of leading others. The majority of the world are followers just looking for a leader. Followers only allow a leader to go so far before they question their direction. Followers do not always like a leader's decisions, and while they may carry out the task, they will grumble about it the whole time. Leaders are responsible for the day-to-day decisions and well-being of those followers. The decisions leaders make should have the best interest of the followers in mind.

When you think of the word leader, what comes to mind? Boss? Most bosses are not leaders because their decisions are based solely on what is best for the company or the stakeholders, not the employees. If you have a boss who considers the interests of his or her employees and does what is best for them, you have truly found a job worth keeping.

Community group? Again, most are not leaders. Community groups, while having a mind-set of growth and betterment of the community as a whole, are mostly there for name recognition and to further their careers.

As for pastors—I have had the privilege of knowing several pastors who show true leadership. They put the well-being of their congregation into every decision. They allow God to be the head of the church and allow His guidance and leadership in everything that happens.

> "Trust in the Lord with all your heart, and lean not on your own understanding; In all your ways acknowledge Him, and He shall direct your paths" (Proverbs 3:5–6).

There are some great leaders in the Bible. One of those is Noah. Noah did not start out as a leader. He was not the commander of a great army. Noah found favor with God in the middle of a corrupt world that God was in despair over. God saw Noah and tasked him with building an ark. Noah was a true leader because he did what was right in the face of adversity. Noah also had to stand alone. There was no reason for Noah to build this ark, but he did it anyway. He did not follow the crowd or succumb to naysayers. Noah prevailed.

> "Thus Noah did; according to all that God commanded him, so he did" (Genesis 6:22).

I wonder if Noah knew when he took that first step how long he would be in the ark. Probably not. What a journey Noah walked with the Lord. There is also much discussion on how many years it took Noah to build the ark. In Genesis 6, before the Lord commands Noah to build the ark, the Lord says that He has numbered the years of man to one hundred and twenty. Noah was five hundred years old when he was tasked with building the ark and six hundred years old when he entered the ark. Others say it took between fifty-five to seventy-five years. Any one of these shows Noah's leadership, his determination and faith. Have you ever stuck with something and been faithful to it for this length of time? If so, you know what Noah went through to complete this task for the Lord. If not, try committing to your service and when you feel like wavering, think of the life of Noah and keep moving forward.

Isaiah is another example of a leader. In Isaiah 6, Isaiah has a vision and hears the voice of the Lord asking who to send. Isaiah immediately volunteers to be sent. He took a stand for the Lord and did what was right for the people. He went.

> "Also I heard the voice of the Lord, saying: "Whom shall I send, and who will go for Us?"
> Then I said, "Here am I! Send me."
> And He said, "Go, and tell this people:
>
> 'Keep on hearing, but do not understand;
> Keep on seeing, but do not perceive.'
> "Make the heart of this people dull,
> and their ears heavy,
> and shut their eyes;
> Lest they see with their eyes,
> and hear with their ears,
> and understand with their heart,
> and return and be healed."
>
> Then I said, "Lord, how long?"
> And He answered:
>
> "Until the cities are laid waste and without inhabitant,
> the houses are without a man,
> the land is utterly desolate,
> the Lord has removed men far away,
> and the forsaken places are many in the midst of the land.
> But yet a tenth will be in it,

and will return and be for consuming,
    as a terebinth tree or as an oak,
    whose stump remains when it is cut down.
    So the holy seed shall be its stump." (Isaiah 6:8–13)

God did not tell Isaiah to only tell his family or his close friends. The Lord said to go and tell the people. Isaiah questioned how long he needed to tell others. The answer was not just today or just when you feel like it. The answer was until there are no inhabitants left. Basically, the remaining years of his life.

We might be agreeable to tell our family and friends because we want them to have what we have and be in heaven with us. But what about people you have never met? People you see on the street. Your neighbors. People in your church. Would you tell them about God? Would you take a stand for the Lord? That is what Isaiah did. He did not know all the people he was called to tell. He answered the call of service to the Lord. He had a heart for others—even those he had never met.

The best example of a leader is found in the life of Jesus. He showed us servant leadership. He never put Himself above others, He always looked out for His disciples, and in the end, when the time came to go to the cross, He washed the disciples' feet.

"Now before the Feast of the Passover, when Jesus knew that His hour had come that He should depart from this world to the Father, having loved His own who were in the world, He loved them to the end. And supper being ended, the devil having already put it into the heart of Judas Iscariot, Simon's son, to betray Him, Jesus, knowing that the Father had given all things into His hands, and that He had come from God and was going to God, rose from supper and laid aside His garments, took a towel and girded Himself.

After that, He poured water into a basin and began to wash the disciples' feet, and to wipe them with the towel with which He was girded. Then He came to Simon Peter. And Peter said to Him, "Lord, are You washing my feet?"

Jesus answered and said to him, "What I am doing you do not understand now, but you will know after this."

Peter said to Him, "You shall never wash my feet!"

Jesus answered him, "If I do not wash you, you have no part with Me."

Simon Peter said to Him, "Lord, not my feet only, but also my hands and my head!"

Jesus said to him, "He who is bathed needs only to wash his feet, but is completely clean; and you are clean, but not all of you." For He knew who would betray Him; therefore He said, "You are not all clean."

So when He had washed their feet, taken His garments, and sat down again, He said to them, "Do you know what I have done to you? You call Me Teacher and Lord, and you say well, for so I am. If I then, your Lord and Teacher, have washed your feet, you also ought to wash one another's feet. For I have given you an example, that you should do as I have done to you. Most assuredly, I say to you, a servant is not greater than his master; nor is he who is sent greater than he who sent him. If you know these things, blessed are you if you do them." (John 13:1–17)

He knew who would betray Him, and He washed Judas's feet anyway. What a picture of servant-leadership. Even though Judas did wrong, Jesus still showed him grace. Do you have a Judas in your life who could use a little grace? I think we all do.

Jesus shows us that no one is greater than another. You can have all the money and status in your community. You can have made a name for yourself throughout this world. If you do not have Jesus as your Lord and Savior, what has it profited you? When you pass from this life and stand before the Lord, will all your worldly possessions mean anything?

If you want to see change, then be the change. If you are unhappy in your workplace, be the light. The light is a leader who shows others that there is a better way. If you want change in your home life, shine your light bright. Stand against adversity. If there is turmoil in your church, look at others through Jesus's eyes. Show love when they expect hate. Show grace when they expect judgment. Show forgiveness when they expect condemnation.

Leadership is not necessarily about being the boss over others. It is about putting others first and showing them the love of Jesus. People will not want a life with God if we do not look different from the world. We have to show them that there is a better way to walk through this life. That better way starts with Jesus.

12

CHURCH

This one is huge. Church is food for the soul. Do not just go to the first church you stop at; that may not be the church God has in mind for you. Pray and ask God to lead you to your church home. There is a difference.

You can go to any church, but if you are not where God wants you, you will not experience the complete plan God has for your life. You can follow your family or friends to their church, but that does not mean their church is your church home.

Going to church and having a church home are completely different. I have been to lots of different churches, and I love worshipping with other believers, but my church home is where I experience growth. It is where I am accepted for exactly who I am and loved unconditionally. You can go to church and have a great time, get excited, and have fun, but unfortunately, that is not true worship. True worship comes from the heart and soul. It is more than a fleeting feeling. It is a lasting relationship. It cements your relationship with God.

God desires that we gather with other believers. The church is that place to gather, to be in one accord, and to work for the glory of the Lord.

"And let us consider one another in order to stir up love and good works, not forsaking the assembling of ourselves together, as is the manner of some, but exhorting one another, and so much the more as you see the Day approaching" (Hebrews 10:24–25).

"For as the body is one and has many members, but all the members of that one body, being many, are one body, so also is Christ. For by one Spirit we were all baptized into one body-whether Jews or Greeks, whether slaves or free-and have all been made to drink into one Spirit. For in fact the body is not one member but many.

If the foot should say, "Because I am not a hand, I am not of the body," is it therefore not of the body? And if the ear should say, "Because I am not an eye, I am not of the body," is it therefore not of the body? If the whole body were an eye, where would be the hearing? If the whole were hearing, where would be the smelling? But now God has set the members, each one of them, in the body just as He pleased. And if they were all one member, where would the body be?

But now indeed there are many members, yet one body. And the eye cannot say to the hand, "I have no need of you"; nor again the head to the feet, "I have no need of you." (1 Corinthians 12:12–21)

Church is a place to fellowship and work together. You can work by yourself for the Lord. There is nothing wrong with that. But when you combine your talents with other believers', the number of people you can reach multiples and you are able to share the load. That is why the church is referred to as a body of believers. Maybe it looks like this: your gifts and talents are the hands, and another believer's gifts and talents are the feet. When they work together, the body functions the way God intended it to. When someone is missing, part of the body is missing, and it does not function as well without that part. When everyone comes together and the body of believers is whole, great things can happen.

> "Now, therefore, you are no longer strangers and foreigners, but fellow citizens with the saints and members of the household of God, having been built on the foundation of the apostles and prophets, Jesus Christ Himself being the chief cornerstone, in whom the whole building, being fitted together, grows into a holy temple in the Lord." (Ephesians 2:19–21)

That is why I say that God has your church home picked out. He sees and knows all. He knows which parts each church is missing, and He leads you to the church where you fit perfectly. A church would not function very well if all its members were called to be pastors.

> "For as we have many members in one body, but all the members do not have the same function, so we, being many, are one body in Christ, and individually members of one another. Having then gifts differing according to the grace that is given to us, let us use them: if prophecy, let us prophesy in proportion to our faith; or ministry, let us use it in our ministering; he who teaches, in teaching; he who exhorts, in exhortation; he who gives, with liberality; he who leads, with diligence; he who shows mercy, with cheerfulness." (Romans 12:4–8)

This also means you have to answer the call that has been placed on your life. If you were called to be a pastor and the church that God leads you to is without a pastor, but you refuse the call, then the body of believers will not function the way God intended them to.

Do not get me wrong, if you refuse the call placed on your life, God will raise someone else up to take that spot. His plan will get accomplished, and you will miss out on the growth and blessing. God has given us free will. That essentially means that if you want to attend another church instead of where God leads you, then God will allow you to do that. You will not experience the fullness of God, nor the life He has planned for you, but that is your choice. God is not going to force you to serve Him. He wants and deserves your service, but you have to be willing to serve Him.

I spent a long time serving God the way I wanted instead of the plan He had for me. I worked so hard for the Lord in the wrong direction. I was involved in everything. Anytime a volunteer was needed, my hand was up. I became so busy working for God, but not with God. There is a huge difference. Nothing I did went like I thought it should. I spent so much time frustrated and feeling defeated. My life and growth with God was stagnant. When I finally stopped long enough to listen, He revealed that my work was for self and not for Him. I was not seeking Him in any of it, and this was not His plan for my life.

Once I changed directions and started just following Him, life became much more fruitful. Yes, I am still busy working for the Lord. But that busyness is not overwhelming or frustrating. It is fulfilling. Nothing I do now feels like work; it feels like service. Every day I want to do more, serve more, and reach more people. If there is a free moment in my day, I want it to be focused on Him and His plans. My life is nothing without the Lord. My service is nothing without His guidance and His leadership. My church attendance is nothing if I am in the wrong place.

A life of abundance is waiting; all you have to do is answer the call.

13

BELIEVERS

When I started following God, I lost a lot of people I thought were my friends. It was not anything any group did. It was the fact that I was different, and just being around me made them uncomfortable. I remember being at an event, and when I walked into the room, people stopped talking and stared at me. As I left the room, they started talking again. I felt out of place; they felt uncomfortable. All because I had chosen a different path. They could see I was not the same person I was before. I remember leaving that event early because I learned that everyone was waiting for me to leave. It was just a sad feeling knowing I no longer fit in.

Then I met other Christians. When we gathered and fellowshipped, it was amazing. This was a group where I fit in. We have amazing times together, and we lean on each other in times of need. The guidance we give is rooted in the Bible, and we bring God into everything we do. We laugh together, cry as a group, and most of all, accept each other. When no one else understands my walk with God, my friends do. They support and encourage me, pray for me, and truly want God's plan for my life. It is an amazing feeling to know you have this type of support system.

"Two are better than one, because they have a good reward for their labor. For if they fall, one will lift up his companion. But woe to him who is alone when he falls, for he has no one to help him up. Again, if two lie down together, they will keep warm; But how can one be warm alone? Though one may be overpowered by another, two can withstand him. And a threefold cord is not quickly broken." (Ecclesiastes 4:9–12)

We can walk with God through this life alone. We can completely lean on God for everything. But the Bible says to surround yourself with other believers. It talks about encouraging one another, praying for one another, and caring for one another. Those words would not be in there if this was not the way God wanted us to live. He never intended anyone to have to be alone. He even made Eve as a companion for Adam. God wants you to surround yourself with a great support system. That support system is other true believers.

Most of us have families, and some of those families are great support systems. If your family are not Christians, there is possibly something missing. It is not their fault that they do not understand what you are going through. They are spiritually discerned until they give their heart and life to God. When that happens, they will truly be able to support your Christian walk.

I have some wonderful family members that I cherish dearly and pray for daily. We will never turn away from each other. Then, I have other family members who have chosen to walk away. I imagine most of us have been in this situation. That is why it is so important to allow God to guide you where you belong.

"Assuredly, I say to you, whatever you bind on earth will be bound in heaven, and whatever you loose on earth will be loosed in heaven.

"Again I say to you that if two of you agree on earth concerning anything that they ask, it will be done for them by My Father in heaven. For where two or three are gathered together in My name, I am there in the midst of them." (Matthew 18:18–20)

Not everyone has a family. Now you do. When you said yes to Jesus, you became part of the family of God. Your new church home—those people are your family. I absolutely love mine, and they are family to me. Your new friends who are true believers in Christ are your family. We are all family. We are brothers and sisters in Christ. You have a support system out there waiting for you. It took a while for me to find mine, but I am so thankful that I did. Keep walking with God and allowing His leadership in your life and you will find yours too.

"And if it seems evil to you to serve the Lord, choose for yourselves this day whom you will serve, whether the gods which your fathers served that were on the other side of the River, or the gods of the Amorites, in whose land you dwell. But as for me and my house, we will serve the Lord." (Joshua 24:15)

When we surround ourselves with other believers, it is easier to stay on course with God. Ever notice that you tend to act like those you hang out with. If you are around people who curse, out of nowhere a curse word pops out of your mouth. If you are around people who party, you go to parties too. If you are around people who speak of God, then you talk about God too. If you do not believe me, test it out. Watch your behavior change based on who you are around. It happens in the workplace, at home, or when you are out.

I think it happens at the workplace the most because we spend so much of our time there. We tend to talk and walk like our coworkers. If you have a job where your coworkers are all Christians, that is wonderful. But the majority of workplaces are not like that. The people we work with might even refer to themselves as Christians, but you will know by the fruit they bear whether that statement is true.

Standing against the current is difficult. I worked in a place where I stood alone. I walked differently from everyone else. It was like walking upstream against the wind. If you are currently in this situation, pray and seek His leadership. Sometimes the answer is to stay, to show others the light of Christ, and to be a witness and help those in need. Other times the answer is to find another job where you will be accepted. I have been in both situations. That is strictly between you and God. If He tells you to stay, it is super important to have that support system outside work to build you up and keep you on track with God.

I realize some will read this and memories of being hurt by other Christians will pop into their heads. Although I would love to say that will never happen, I know too well that is not the case. This is why I have stressed to seek the Lord's guidance and follow His direction. Just because you live next door to a church does not make that your church home. Just because the people at work claim to be Christians does not make them your support system.

Not all Christians are the same. People have very different views on what it takes to have eternal life. The Bible is extremely clear on this. John 14:6 says Jesus is the only way. Once we surrender our lives to Him and root His Word in our hearts, we are like the good soil.

> "Then He spoke many things to them in parables, saying: "Behold, a sower went out to sow. And as he sowed, some seed fell by the wayside; and the birds came and devoured them. Some fell on stony places, where they did not have much earth; and they immediately sprang up because they had no depth of earth. But when the sun was up they were scorched, and because they had no root they withered away.

And some fell among thorns, and the thorns sprang up and choked them. But others fell on good ground and yielded a crop: some a hundredfold, some sixty, some thirty. He who has ears to hear, let him hear!" (Matthew 13:3–9)

"Therefore hear the parable of the sower: When anyone hears the word of the kingdom, and does not understand it, then the wicked one comes and snatches away what was sown in his heart. This is he who received seed by the wayside. But he who received the seed on stony places, this is he who hears the word and immediately receives it with joy; yet he has no root in himself, but endures only for a while. For when tribulation or persecution arises because of the word, immediately he stumbles. Now he who received seed among the thorns is he who hears the word, and the cares of this world and the deceitfulness of riches choke the word, and he becomes unfruitful. But he who received seed on the good ground is he who hears the word and understands it, who indeed bears fruit and produces: some a hundredfold, some sixty, some thirty." (Matthew 13:18–23)

There are those who claim to be Christians but have never had a heart conversion. The Word is not rooted in them; they only serve with their minds and not their hearts. Always remember that what these people do is not a reflection on God and His love for you. They simply do not have the love of God in their hearts and they need your prayers. Strive to be the seed in the good soil that bears fruit for the Lord.

14

FELLOWSHIP

The Greek word *koinonia* means Christian fellowship or body of believers. Christians have shared beliefs, convictions, and values. When those come together, we experience genuine koinonia. When the body of believers is in accord, great things happen for the Kingdom of God. With so much strife in the world, it is refreshing to step into a situation where there is peace and harmony.

The other night at church we had testimony time, and I listened as each person talked about how amazing God had been in his or her life that day. The absolute joy in their voices and awe-inspiring testimonials lifted my spirit—to see God at work around me in each person's life. To hear about God meeting them at their need and being their guiding light warmed my heart.

I am thankful that I get the opportunity to fellowship with other believers. Maybe I had a hard or discouraging day and I walk in to hear about God and His work. My whole attitude changes. Life is not that bad anymore. Whatever I am going through is just a bump in the road. I need to get back up and keep moving forward. That is the value of fellowship.

The sociological aspect of it is that as humans, we need social interaction. We look forward to those times of being around others. God saw that man was lonely, even though he had a relationship with the Lord. God saw that it was not good for man to be alone. God did not make man to be alone. We were made to be together. He made woman to keep him company and be his helpmate. People are made to fellowship with other people.

> "As iron sharpens iron, so a man sharpens the countenance of his friend. Whoever keeps the fig tree will eat its fruit; so he who waits on his master will be honored. As in water face reflects face, so a man's heart reveals the man." (Proverbs 27:17–19)

There is something so sweet about Christian fellowship. We have met some wonderful Christian brothers and sisters over the years. My family has been so blessed with a group of people who encourage and lift each other up. People who are truly impacted by our Christian walk. What a blessing to know those who love people like Christ loves us. They see a need and fill it. They minister to those around them. They pray with others and lift up their burdens. Whole congregations set aside time to pray for someone so they are all in one accord.

At our church we do what I call the circle prayer, where we all come together and hold on to each other and pray specifically. Someone will call for the circle prayer and everyone immediately leaves their seats and joins together, lifting up the prayer. That is the value of fellowship. Maybe we are not all righteous that day, but because we pray together, the fervent one, the one who is righteous is praying beside you. That prayer avails much.

I am not sure like-mindedness is a word, but it should be. Fellowship between Christians means you know the people around you are like-minded. They follow the same God you do and read the Bible just like you. You can express things to them that the rest of the world might not understand. The direction that God has pointed me to travel, at times, only my Christian brothers and sisters understood. Some of my decisions and reasoning that this was the path God had for me have been met with some pretty confused faces. Not being able to explain beyond that puts them at a disadvantage for understanding. There have been many times during my walk with God that I did not know where I was going, so I could not explain it to others. My "all in" philosophy when it comes to God's calling has led to some very perplexed looks and interesting conversations. I have been told I am not normal, which is fine since I do not believe there is a normal. The rationale that everyone should be the same and act the same does not make sense to me. That there is some imaginary standard that we should all be measured by does not line up with the Bible. God made each of us unique with our own characteristics and attributes so that we could stand out and be leaders, leading others to Him. God gave each of us different gifts and talents so that we fit together in the Body of Christ. None of that sounds like the world's definition of normal. If I spent a lot of time looking into the world's definition of who I should be, I guess this would be my turn to have the perplexed face. But I know who I am and Who I belong to. I am a child of God. Created for a purpose. Created in His image. Created to have a relationship with Him. Created to be loved by God. What a privilege to be part of His world.

> "This is the message which we have heard from Him and declare to you, that God is light and in Him is no darkness at all. If we say that we have fellowship with Him, and walk in darkness, we lie and do not practice the truth. But if we walk in the light as He is in the light, we have fellowship with one another, and the blood of Jesus Christ His Son cleanses us from all sin. If we say that we have no sin, we deceive ourselves, and the truth is not in us. If we confess our sins, He is faithful and just to forgive us our sins and to cleanse us from all unrighteousness." (1 John 1:5–9)

When we stand together, there is understanding and unity. When we are in one accord, it is a blessing. We put ourselves and our differences aside so that we can work together with a common purpose. We all need that in our Christian walk. It gives us a chance to learn, grow, and strengthen our faith. Fellowship is food for our souls. Fellowship with other believers strengthens our walk with God.

WELCOME!

You have made the best decision of your life. You are part of the family of God. Congratulations on your new life and walk with God! As you have read through these pages, it is my hope that you have found direction, peace, and grace.

Life is about moments and steps—moments show you how truly blessed this life is, and steps grow your relationship with God. Thank you for walking through this book with me. It is my prayer that you can take what you have learned and apply it to your life with God. That your walk will be deliberate and steadfast. I am so proud of you. Continue moving forward and continue to grow in grace with your Lord and Savior. Take each day as it comes and each step one at a time.

REFERENCES

Ball, S. (2003) A Christian Physicist Examines the Big Bang Theory. *LeTourneau University* https://www.letu.edu/academics/arts-and-sciences/files/big-bang.pdf

Thayer and Smith. (1999) Greek Lexicon entry for Baptizo. *The NAS New Testament Greek Lexicon.* https://www.biblestudytools.com/lexicons/greek/nas/baptizo.html

Williams, M. (2015) What Is the Big Bang Theory? *Universe Today* www.phys.org/news/2015-12-big-theory.html.

Bible Gateway (1982) Thomas Nelson. https://www.biblegateway.com/.

Bible Gateway was often used to cite scripture.

ABOUT THE AUTHOR

Joye Angel is the founder of Hands Outstretched for People Everywhere (HOPE) ministries, an author, blogger, and host of the Road of Faith podcast. She and her husband, Kevin, have three amazing adult children and reside in Oklahoma. Joye enjoys writing, spending time with family, and sharing God's love with others. For more, visit www.joyelangel.com or www.myhopeministries.com.

Printed in the United States
by Baker & Taylor Publisher Services